UNDER EVERY TREE

A Guide to Finding Your Roots in Virginia

Phyllis Brock Silber

Foreword by Conley L. Edwards, III

Author: Phyllis Silber

Graphic Designer: Amy Mendelson Design, Amy Mendelson Cheeley

Publisher: Dementi Milestone Publishing, Manakin-Sabot, VA
          with the full support of The Richmond Times-Dispatch,
          Richmond, VA

Cover Art: Susan Shadis

ISBN: 9780996915755

Library of Congress Control Number: 2016931946

Printed in the USA

County Courthouses on cover L-R: Warren; Carroll; Goochland; Nottoway; Fairfax

DEDICATION

This book is dedicated to the memory of my parents,
Ruth Story Brock and Alexander Bige Brock
And to the future of their descendants:
Janet, Susan
Amanda, Elizabeth, Matthew, Lauren, Gideon,
Nicholas, Benjamin, Katherine, Megan, Brock,
Jasper, Lela, Kaitlin, Riley, Elaine, and Everett

ABOUT THE AUTHOR

Phyllis Silber has been the Executive Director of the Goochland County Historical Society since May of 2000. Phyllis retired from the Montgomery County, Maryland school system as a high school science teacher. She holds graduate degrees from the University of Tennessee and the University of Maryland. She can trace her maternal and paternal roots back to Goochland County in 1735.

"Southerners are so devoted to genealogy that we see a family tree under every bush."

– Florence King

TABLE OF CONTENTS

FOREWORD

Years ago, a colleague in the archives at the Library of Virginia encountered an excited and breathless researcher who had just arrived from the Midwest. After providing some research direction, my colleague whispered to me, "You know, I think finding out that one of your ancestors is from Virginia sells more gasoline than Exxon." Little did we realize that the years that followed would see a growing number of visitors determined to find their Virginia ancestors. Alex Haley's Roots, the increased use of computer technology to index records, digitization of original materials, and consolidation of archival resources by commercial providers would add to the growth of interest in genealogy and family history. While these advances made the resources for family research more readily available, there were still those with the desire to see the original records themselves, to talk with longtime residents of the community, and to walk the land where their ancestors lived and died.

It is obvious that Phyllis Silber has encountered many of those who desired to go straight to the source among local records. In this volume, she does all of us a service by providing detailed directions to the most helpful resources in each locality. Surely from her own experience, she has learned that researchers do not spend their entire time pouring over old records in record rooms, historical societies, or libraries. They have time to visit local points of interest as well and add to the local economy as a result. The reader will find valuable suggestions for places to visit: historic homes and sites, museums, battlefields, parks and hiking trails, churches and cemeteries. Who could pass up an opportunity to visit a whale display at the Caroline County Visitor's Center or the Dip Dog Drive-In in Smyth County?

Pack *Under Every Tree* with your essential research materials. Put it in the glove compartment of your car. Head out. And, good luck with your research among Virginia's rich documentary heritage.

Conley L. Edwards
Retired State Archivist of Virginia

ABOUT CONLEY L. EDWARDS

A member of the staff of the Library of Virginia since August 1974, Conley has served at many levels of management in the Library of Virginia and from January 1996 until November 2009 as State Archivist of Virginia and Director of both the Archival and Information Services Division and the Archival and Records Management Services Division, Library of Virginia. He retired in November 2009 after 35 years of state service. He is currently president of the Friends of the Virginia State Archives and a Governor-at-Large of the Virginia Genealogical Society.

As State Archivist, he served as the Chairman of the Virginia Board for Geographic Names and coordinator for the Virginia State Historical Records Advisory Board. He is a past president of the Council of State Archivists, an organization representing state archivists throughout the US. In April 2007, he received the Patrick Henry Award for leadership in the public interest from his alma mater, Hampden-Sydney College.

ACKNOWLEDGEMENTS

"Uneasy lies the head that wears the crown."

-Henry IV, Part II.III.i.1735

My first thank you goes out to all the Clerks and Deputy Clerks of the Circuit Courts of Virginia for caring so much about the important and fragile records of our history that are in your charge. It was heartwarming to meet so many of you and recognize the familiar passion you have for your job. In my position as director of the Goochland County Histotical Society, I have had many opportunities to work not only with local clerks, but with directors and volunteers at other local historical societies; I am always impressed with their dedication and creativity in pursuit of some nugget of information. I trust this book will in some way repay their good efforts.

Thank you to everyone who read each page, made improvements, and corrected mistakes. Your help made this endeavor so much better. I want to name each librarian, Society director, and friend who helped with the edits but I would undoubtedly overlook someone. Still, if there are errors within these pages, the responsibility is all mine.

Lastly, one does not undertake a task of this magnitude without the support of one's family. My husband has shown great patience as he drove and stopped and drove and stopped. Each time we headed out on a journey to another state, there was always a detour we needed to take in order to catch one more record room in one more county. I am eternally grateful. Then to my two sisters whose encouragement was boundless, I offer a sincere Tennessee "thanks y'all." Mother and Daddy would be tickled, I think.

The Author

HOW TO USE THIS BOOK

Visiting any place to do genealogy research for the first time can be a bit daunting in its own right. Add to that the additional unknowns of where should one go first: a courthouse, library, or historical society, and a person might give up before he gets started! This guide will help. It provides driving, and parking directions and a suggested visit-here-first for each county in the Commonwealth. Instructions for doing research in a county record room follow this introduction.

There are counties in Virginia that no longer exist as a county but have been absorbed into a major city. Information about those former counties can be found in a separate section at the end of the book. They were not included in the main part of the book.

BEFORE YOU GO

Give some thought to what you hope to find on this visit. Make notes if necessary. I've had someone walk in and ask for information on the Parrishes, the Pleasants, and the Pryors which happen to be 3 of the largest families in Goochland. It is okay to ask for one person from 3 different families but one at a time please. Here are some goals to set for yourself before you start out.

- Choose the oldest (earliest) target person that you are for certain is in your family line. It is virtually impossible to begin at Jamestown and work backwards.
- Have specific goals such as identifying a target's parent, finding a grave, or locating their land.
- As important as it may be to you, please keep the discussion of your entire tree for another day. Often volunteers have many other duties and time to help you may be limited.
- Always ask before you photograph or scan photos or documents.
- It is appreciated if you leave a donation if you have spent a lot of time at the Historical Society. (Except for paying for copies this does not apply to the Clerk's office!)

And finally while you are visiting a county, take to time to visit some of the places I've suggested. It will add to your appreciation of the place where your ancestor grew up and will perhaps draw those family ties a bit tighter.

1

USING THE RECORD ROOM AT THE COUNTY COURTHOUSE

Note: *The Record Room will always be near the Clerk's Offices*

The following guidance was originally written by George E. Hoots, III (1940- 2004) Circuit Court Judge, 25th Judicial Circuit, Commonwealth of Virginia. He prepared it for use in Botetourt County. The guidance has been edited by this author for use in all Virginia localities. It is being with permission of the Circuit Court Clerk of Botetourt County.

Marriage Register contains the names of brides and grooms. Each register is indexed in a separate index book. Depending on the time of marriage you may find ages and occupations of bride and groom, occupations, where and when married, and by whom married and the parents' names.

Registers of Births and Deaths: From 1853 to about 1870, these books listed the names of children, the names of the parents, and dates of birth and the names of persons who died, date of death, sometimes cause of death, occupation and names of parents as well as who reported the death. Sometimes these records are very incomplete but worth a look.

Deed Books contain records for conveyance of lands. The persons who sell or convey the lands are called **Grantors** and the buyers or persons receiving the lands are called **Grantees**. Each deed is indexed in both a Grantor and Grantee Index Book. Often when a person died without a will (and sometimes with a will), that person's heirs would sell the property. Deeds also tell you much about where a person may have lived and how much property the person owned.

Will Books (probate records) contain estate records from 1770 to the present. These are important sources of information about when a person died, who the heirs are and what the person may have owned. People who died without a will are said to have died *intestate*, and if there was an administration of their estate, those records are also found in the Will Books. In more recent years, whoever executed the will or administered the estate has been required to give a List of Heirs - the person's next of kin, usually the surviving spouse and children or grandchildren.

There are books that contain official orders of the Circuit Court, the County Court, and the Superior Court (early name of the Circuit Court):

Law Order Books contain the records of suits for money, appointment to county offices and other information.

Chancery Order Books contain records pertaining to divorces, the division (partition) of land, and suits involving relief other than a money judgment. Both sets of books are indexed either in an **Index** book or in the individual book. Many counties now have an index to Chancery suits on-line at the Library of Virginia.

Criminal Order Books contain orders for all criminal cases heard in the Circuit Court which hears both misdemeanor appeals and many cases.

County Court Order Books and Minute Books contain the records of the actions of the County Court which was both a court of law and the governing body of the county.

Surveyor Books show plats of lands surveyed and lists the names of the persons for whom the lands were surveyed. They may literally put your ancestor on the map.

Learn to think phonetically. Clerks often spelled names the way they sound. This creates a real problem especially with ancestors with German names: Zirkle became Circle; Obenshain is in the records as Obenschain, Obenchain, Openchain, Ovenchain, even Oglechain;

Be glad you aren't in Pennsylvania, because the correct spelling of that name is: Abendschonn! Ebershol became Eversole in most places, but here the name is spelled Aversole. The German "d", "p" and t" became almost interchangeable. Remember the word "Dollar" came from a German coin called the "Toler". Other names, such as O'Neil may become over time simply Neil, or McLean may become McClean or Maclean.

When you read handwritten documents, remember these things: punctuation was not well used and some sentences seem to run on forever. Words will be divided at the end of the line irrespective of whether the division makes sense or not. You may see the word "Inhabitant" divided as "inha-bitant". And one of the hardest things to adjust to is letter formation. For instance a word with a double ss, such as "possess" is written to look to us as if it is spelled "pofsefs". You'll find other words we don't use any more: a widow may be called a "relic", a horse is often referred to as "horse-beast", and land measurements are often given in "poles" or "rods" (they both mean the same thing and are 16.5 feet in length). Money is stated in amounts down to the half cent, so something may be valued at $10.12 ½. Money is also given in pounds, shillings and pence. There were 12 pence in a shilling and 20 shillings in a pound. A Virginia pound was worth $53.33, so a shilling was worth 16 ½ cents and a pence was worth 1 ⅓ cents.

Judge Honts authored and co-authored several historical and genealogical publications. He was co-author of *Following the McClures, Donegal to Botetourt; The Brughs of Early Botetourt, 1790; The Paper Mills of Botetourt-County; The Descendants of Jacob Hons/ Jacob John;* and *"The Blue Ridge Rifles,"* as related by the unit's 1st Sgt. J.K. Simmons.

VIRGINIA COUNTIES WITH LOST RECORDS

This is a list of Virginia counties that have incomplete records from the time the county was formed. Because of the near loss of records in Botetourt County in 1970, the General Assembly passed the Virginia Public Records Act in 1975 for the purpose of preserving local records.

Accomack One of the original shires recognized in 1634, it became part of Northampton County in 1643, reverted to Accomack about 1663, merged into Northampton again in October 1670, and reverted to Accomack for a final time in November 1673. A significant number of loose records from the 1700s suffered extreme water and pest damage. Volumes that record deeds, court orders, and wills exist.

Albemarle 1744. All order books except the first and many loose papers between 1748 and 1781 were destroyed by British General Banastre Tarleton's raid on Charlottesville in 1781 during the Revolutionary War.

Appomattox 1845. All records except land tax books were destroyed by fire on 1 February 1892.

Bland 1861. Most loose records were destroyed by fire in 1888. All volumes (Deeds and Wills) and part of the chancery papers were saved.

Botetourt Created by an act of 1769 to take effect on 13 February 1770. Many of the loose records including pre-1830 chancery and pre-1854 judgments suffered tremendous water damage as a result of a courthouse fire on 15 December 1970. Volumes that record deeds, court orders, and wills exist.

Brunswick 1720 (county government established in June 1732). Most loose records prior to 1781 are missing. Pre-1781 volumes that record deeds, court orders, and wills exist.

Buchanan 1858. Records were destroyed in April 1885 by a fire that started at a nearby store; records created after that date suffered extreme damage in a flood in 1977.

Buckingham 1761. Most all records were destroyed by fire in 1869.

Caroline 1728. Most loose records and deed books prior to 1836 and will books prior to 1853 were stolen, mutilated, and/or destroyed by Union troops who ransacked the courthouse in May 1864. A near-complete run of order books exists.

Charles City 1634 an original shire. Records have been destroyed at various times. The most damage occurred during the Civil War when the records were strewn through the woods in a rainstorm. A few pre–Civil War volumes such as deed books, will books, minute books, and order books exist.

Craig 1851. Deed Book A and most of the loose papers were destroyed during a raid in the Civil War. Pre– Civil War recorded deeds were rerecorded in Deed Books B and C. Volumes that record court orders and wills exist.

Culpeper 1749. A significant number of loose records are missing for the period prior to 1840. They were stolen, mutilated, and/ or destroyed during the Civil War. Culpeper was the site of several military engagements and experienced widespread pillaging by both Union and Confederate troops. Volumes that record deeds and wills from the formation of the county exist. Minute books for the periods 1749–1762, 1765–1797, 1812–1813, and 1817 are missing.

Dinwiddie 1752. The bulk of court records prior to 1865 were stolen, mutilated, and/or destroyed by Union troops who ransacked the courthouse during the last months of the Civil War. Post- 1830 volumes such as deed books, will books, chancery order books, and marriage registers exist.

Elizabeth City 1634 an original shire. Records were burned and/or destroyed during the Revolutionary War and the War of 1812. Additional records were burned in Richmond on 3 April 1865, where they had been moved for safekeeping during the Civil War. A few pre–Civil War volumes such as deed books, will books, and order books exist.

Fairfax 1742. Original wills and deeds as well as many other loose papers were destroyed during the Civil War; deed books for twenty-six of the fifty-six years between 1763 and 1819 are missing. Numerous pre–Civil War minute books are missing as well.

Gloucester 1651. All records were destroyed by an 1820 fire, and most of the records created after 1820 were destroyed by fire in Richmond on 3 April 1865, where they had been moved for safekeeping during the Civil War.

Greene 1838. Deed Book 1, 1838–1841, was lost during the Civil War. Some court records, primarily volumes, suffered water damage as a result of a courthouse fire on 24 October 1979.

Hanover created by an act of 1720 to take effect on 1 May 1721. Most county court records, particularly deeds, wills, and marriage records, were destroyed by fire in Richmond on 3 April 1865, where they had been moved for safekeeping during the Civil War. The circuit court records were not moved to Richmond and were relatively unscathed. Many common law papers and chancery papers after 1831 still exist.

Henrico 1634 as an original shire. All county court records prior to 1655 and almost all prior to 1677 are missing. Many records were destroyed by British troops during the Revolutionary War. Post–Revolutionary War county court records exist. Almost all circuit superior court of law and chancery and circuit court records were destroyed by fire in the Civil War. The county's circuit court held its sessions at the state courthouse in Richmond.

Isle of Wight Recognized as Warrosquyoake County, one of the original shires, in 1634 and given its present name in 1637. Most pre–Revolutionary War–era loose records are missing. Volumes that record deeds, court orders, and wills exist.

James City County / Williamsburg 1634 an original shire. Williamsburg was founded in 1699 and declared a "city Incorporate" by a royal charter in 1722, although its actual status was that of a borough. Beginning in 1770, the courts of James City County and Williamsburg shared a common courthouse. During the Civil War, the records of both localities were transferred to Richmond for safekeeping but were destroyed by fire there in Richmond on 3 April 1865. The records of the Superior Court of Chancery for the Williamsburg district were destroyed by a courthouse fire in April 1911.

King and Queen 1691. Records were lost in courthouse fires in 1828 and 1833. Records were again destroyed by a courthouse fire set by Union troops on 10 March 1864 during the Civil War.

King George Created by an act of 1720 to take effect on 19 May in 1721. Most loose records prior to 1830 are missing. Volumes that record deeds, court orders, and wills exist.

King William by an act of 1701 to take effect on 11 April 1702. Most records were destroyed by a courthouse fire on 17 January 1885. Only a few order books and deed books exist.

Lee County Created in 1792 to take effect on 13 May 1793. A significant number of loose records prior to 1860 including chancery and judgments are missing. Most volumes including deed books, will books, and order books exist.

Mathews by an act of 1790 to take effect on 1 May 1791. Most records were burned in Richmond on 3 April 1865, where they had been moved for safekeeping during the Civil War.

Mecklenburg 1764. Numerous loose records prior to 1783 are missing. Volumes that record deeds, court orders, and wills exist.

Middlesex 1669. Numerous loose records from the nineteenth century including chancery, judgments, and commonwealth causes are missing. Most volumes including deed books, will books, and order books exist.

Nansemond called Upper Norfolk County by 1640 and renamed Nansemond in 1646. Records were destroyed in three separate fires: the earliest consumed the house of the court clerk in April 1734, the second was set by British troops in 1779, and the last occurred on 7 February 1866.

New Kent 1654. Records were destroyed when John Posey set fire to the courthouse on 15 July 1787. Many records were lost when the courthouse was partially destroyed by fire during Civil War hostilities in 1862. Additional records were burned in Richmond on 3 April 1865.

Northumberland 1645. The county suffered some losses in a fire in the clerk's office on 25 October 1710. Volumes beginning in 1650 that record deeds, court orders, and wills exist.

Nottoway by an act of 1788 to take effect on 1 May 1789. Many records were destroyed or heavily mutilated in 1865 by Union troops during the Civil War. A few volumes that record deeds, court orders, and wills exist.

Prince George by an act of 1702 to take effect on 23 April 1703. Most court records were destroyed in 1782 by British troops during the Revolutionary War and again in 1864 by Union troops during the Civil War. A few volumes that record deeds, court orders, and wills exist.

Prince William by an act of 1730 to take effect on 1 March 1731. Many pre–Civil War records were lost, destroyed, or stolen by Union troops in 1863 during the Civil War. Sixteen deed books and five will books are missing.

Richmond (City) Established in 1742 and incorporated as a town, in 1782 it officially became the City of Richmond. During the burning of Richmond efforts were made to save the circuit court records found at the State Court House. All the papers that were necessary to pending suits and many of the order books were saved, but all of the wills and deed books were lost. Records of the superior court and circuit superior court of law and chancery were also destroyed. Most of the pre–Civil War Hustings Court records exist.

Richmond County 1692. Some volumes were burned and mutilated through unknown causes; in addition, the will books prior to 1699 were missing as early as 1793, and order books for the period 1794–1816 are also missing. Numerous loose records prior to 1781 are missing as well.

Rockingham 1778. A courthouse fire in 1787 destroyed primarily wills and estate records. In June 1864 during the Civil War, court records (mostly volumes) were removed from the courthouse and loaded on a wagon to be taken to a place of safety on or beyond the Blue Ridge. Many order books, deed books, will books, and fiduciary books, however, were lost or severely damaged by the fire. The loose records that remained at the courthouse were undamaged. Pre-1865 records including deeds and wills were rerecorded following an act of assembly passed in November 1884.

Russell 1786. The first marriage register and most loose papers were lost in a fire in the clerk's office in 1872. Volumes that record deeds, court orders, and wills (except Will Book 1) exist.

Spotsylvania created by an act of 1720 to take effect on 1 May 1721. Many loose county court papers prior to 1839, when the courthouse moved from Fredericksburg to Spotsylvania Courthouse, are missing. Volumes that record deeds, court orders, and wills exist. The district court, superior court, and circuit court records of Spotsylvania County from 1813 to 1889 are in Fredericksburg.

Stafford 1664. Many pre–Civil War court records were lost to vandalism by Union troops during the Civil War. A few volumes that record deeds, court orders, and wills exist.

Surry 1652. Deed Book 10 (1835–1838) is missing and order books for 1718–1741 and various other early volumes are fragmentary. Most loose records prior to 1806 are missing. Courthouse fires in 1906 and 1922, however, did not result in loss of records, which were then housed in a separate clerk's office.

Warwick recognized as Warwick River County, one of the original shires, in 1634; the name was shortened to Warwick in 1643. County court records were destroyed at several times with most destruction occurring during the Civil War. The clerk's office was burned on 15 December 1864. County court minute books and loose records from 1787 to 1819 were destroyed by the fire. Additional records were burned in Richmond on 3 April 1865, where they had been moved for safekeeping during the Civil War.

Washington by an act of 1776, court first met on 18 January 1777. Minute books for the periods 1787–1819 and 1821–1837 and many loose papers were lost on 15 December 1864 when the courthouse was burned during Stoneman's Raid. The fire was set by Union captain James B. Wyatt of the 13th Tennessee Cavalry. Wyatt, who was raised in Washington County, sought revenge for what he claimed was a wrong done against him by a county court judge before the war.

Westmoreland 1653. Many loose papers were burned during both the Revolutionary War and the Civil War. Volumes that record deeds, court orders (except for an order book for the period 1764–1776), and wills exist.

York Recognized in 1634 as an original shire. Most pre– Revolutionary War–era loose records are missing. Volumes that record deeds, court orders, and wills do exist.

THE LIBRARY OF VIRGINIA

In 1823 the General Assembly of Virginia created a state library to be known as The Library of Virginia. Its mission: *"As the Commonwealth's library and archives, the Library of Virginia is a trusted educational institution. We acquire, preserve, and promote access to unique collections of Virginia's history and culture and advance the development of library and records management services statewide."* The Library was housed in the Capitol building in Richmond for almost 75 years. In 1895 and again in 1940 the Library moved to new locations near Capital Square. In 1997 the Library moved into to its current home at 800 East Broad Street. *"The Library houses the most comprehensive collection of materials on Virginia government, history, and culture available anywhere. The collections illustrate the rich and varied past of the commonwealth, documenting the lives of Virginians whose deeds are known to all, as well as those of ordinary citizens whose accomplishments are the foundation of our heritage."* (quotes taken from lva.virginia.gov)

 ## WHERE TO START

If you are just beginning a journey into your family history, or if you have limited time for research in Virginia, this is by far the best place to begin. You will have information about every county in the Commonwealth at your disposal. There are family files and indices to early genealogy journals. Magazines on the shelves with family histories are just waiting for you to discover information about that illusive ggg grandfather. My only caveat is to allow plenty of time and arrive early for free parking! These directions will assume travel from outside the city.

FIND IT: 800 East Broad Street, Richmond, VA 23219
From I-95 north or south, exit #74C. Follow it up and around to the right (east) onto Broad Street at 13th Street. Broad Street is one-way. Move into the right lane and turn right onto 9th Street. Move into the far left lane as the parking garage entrance is just ahead on the left. Turn left and left again to the ticket kiosk. An elevator will take you up to street level. Exit and then enter the library through

the glass doors on the right. Be sure to get your ticket validated at the front desk before you leave. Walk up the stairs to the second level and check in at the desk. **(804) 692.3500 lva.virginia.gov**

Basic Genealogical Resources at the Library of Virginia

Census Records: The first U.S. census was taken in 1790 and a census has been taken every 10 years since. The censuses and indexes for Virginia for 1790, 1800, part of 1810, and 1890 have not survived. From 1850, the census lists the names of all individuals in the household on the day the census was taken.

Vital Records: 1853–1896 birth and death registers, 1913–1939 death certificates, and 1853–1935 marriage registers are available at the Library of Virginia. Marriages prior to June 1853 were recorded at the local courthouse.

County and City Records: Deeds, wills, court records, marriages, and other types of documents recorded at the local level of government will be found in the individual courthouses of Virginia's counties and independent cities. The Library of Virginia has microfilm copies of the surviving court records prior to 1865.

Military Records: The Library has microfilm copies of military muster rolls, service records, and/or pension records for most Virginia soldiers who served during the colonial wars, the American Revolution, the War of 1812, and the Civil War. World War I History Commission questionnaires contain biographical information about some World War I veterans living in Virginia after the war.

Bible Records: Bible records primarily consist of photocopies of original family registers found in Bibles. There also are typed transcripts and some compilations of Bible records by patriotic organizations such as the Daughters of the American Revolution.

Genealogical Notes and Charts: This collection consists of a wide variety of materials compiled by private citizens. The information contained therein has not been verified.

Compiled by Carolyn H. Goudie and Virginia S. Dunn Revised 2002 Reprinted 2008

THE LIBRARY OF VIRGINIA
(Continued)

Examples of LVA Basic Checklist of Genealogy Resource Sites and Research Guides

African American Research
Cavaliers and Pioneers
Cemeteries
Chalkley's Chronicles
Chancery Cases
Colonial Wars Bounty Lands
Colonial Tithables
Early Virginia Marriage Records
18th Century VA Newspapers
Genealogical Records at LVA
Headrights
Judgments
Kentucky Records at LVA
Mutual Assurance Society Records
Northern Neck Land Proprietary Records
Poll Books
The Archives Collections
Virginia Place Names
Soldiers of the War of 1812
Stewart's Index to Printed Genealogies
Taxes in Colonial Virginia
Tithables
Using County and City Court Records; Land Tax Records;
     Personal Property Tax Records
Using Women's History Resources
Using the Virginia Historical Index (Swem)
Using Virginia Civil War Records
Using Virginia Governors' Records, 1776-1998
Using Virginia Revolutionary War Records
Using Vital Statistics Records

The Virginia Colonial Records Project

Virginia, Discovered and Described: John Smith's Map of Virginia and Its Derivatives

Virginia Land Office - Research Notes Number 20

Virginia Naturalizations, 1657-1776

Virginia Naturalizations, 1776-1900

The Virginia Writers' Project

West Virginia Records

Examples of Bibliographies

Clemency Records

Coal Mining Camps: Records and Resources

Historic Virginia Documents on the Internet

Hollywood Cemetery: Selected Resources

The Internal Improvement Movement in Virginia: Early Canals, River Navigations, Roads, Turnpikes, Bridges and Railroads

Jamestown and Seventeenth-Century Colonial Virginia: A Selection of Readings and Web Sites

John Brown's Raid: Records and Resources

Organization Records at the Library of Virginia

Resources on Native Americans: Archival Sources and Published Materials

Selected Bibliography of Map Books and Periodicals, Many of which Relate to Virginia

Selected Civil War Resources in the Personal Papers and Military Records Collections

Selected Indexing of Virginia Newspapers

Slavery in Virginia

Sources on Patrick Henry

Virginia Company History Sources

Virginia Women and the First World War: Records and Resources

Virginia Women and the Second World War: Records and Resources at the Library of Virginia

The WRVA Radio Collection

ACCOMACK COUNTY

Accomac Shire was established by the House of Burgesses in 1634 as one of the original eight shires of Virginia. In 1642 the county name was changed to Northampton. Northampton was then split into two counties in 1663. The northern area was renamed Accomack County. According to the U.S. Census Bureau, the county is the largest in Virginia. The county seat is Accomac.

 ## WHERE TO START

FAMILY RESEARCH

Eastern Shore Public Library: The researcher will find a large collection of primary and secondary sources. The Miles files and the Mears Collection are available through the library's website.

> **FIND IT: 23610 Front Street, Accomac, VA. 23301** From the Chesapeake Bay Tunnel drive about 55 miles north on US 13/ Lankford Hwy. Turn right (east) onto US 13 Bus/ Front Street. Travel 1.3 miles to the Library ahead on the right.
> **(757) 787.3400 espl.org**

ORIGINAL DOCUMENTS

Accomack County Clerk of the Circuit Court has court records that exist from 1663.

> **FIND IT: 23316 Courthouse Ave, Accomac, VA 23301**
> From the Library turn back west on Front Street. In .5 mi turn right (north) onto Court House Avenue. Park on the street. The Clerk's Office entrance is to the left of the main Courthouse entrance. It is about a 15 minute walk from the Library.
> **(757) 787.5776**

GOOD TO KNOW

10 miles north of the Bay Tunnel on the Eastern Shore is the town of
Cape Charles, VA. The Historical Society of Cape Charles maintains
a museum with a rich collection of early postcards, photographs,
timetables, documents, and objects which details Cape Charles in the
1880s. Take U.S. 13 and follow signs to Cape Charles, located about 10
miles north of the entrance (exit) to the Chesapeake Bay Bridge Tunnel.
Go west on State Route 184. The Museum is 1.8 miles from the
intersection of Rt. 13 and Rt. 184, a tall brick building on the south
(left) side of the road as you enter the town, just past the water tower.
(757) 331.1008 **smallmuseum.org/capechas**

At the north end of the Eastern Shore are Chincoteague, and Assateague
Islands. Wallops Flight Facility, a NASA space launch base, is located at
Chincoteague. Tangier Island, and Smith Island, off the western shore in
the Chesapeake Bay, are additional destinations reached by daily ferries.
Blackwater Wildlife Refuge 2145 Key Wallace Drive, Cambridge, MD 21613
If you have a passion for birding and wildlife, a two hour drive into
Maryland from Accomac will be worth the effort. A beautiful Visitor
Center, a Wildlife Drive, hiking trails, paddling trails, and miles of
cycling roads can be found here. The Refuge is unique in that it hosts the
largest remaining natural population of Delmarva fox squirrels and is also
host to the largest breeding population of bald eagles on the East Coast,
north of Florida. **(410) 228.2677** **fws.gov/blackwater**

ALBEMARLE COUNTY

Albemarle County was formed from Goochland County in 1744. Albemarle County was named in honor of Willem Anne van Keppel, 2nd Earl of Albemarle. The county seat is Charlottesville.

WHERE TO START

FAMILY RESEARCH

Albemarle Charlottesville Historical Society: This is the best place to begin. The librarian is very knowledgeable as are the volunteers and all are willing to help the researcher. The Society has extensive family files and a large library which includes sources from many of the counties in the Commonwealth. Plan to stay a while.

> **FIND IT: 200 Second Street NE, Charlottesville, VA 22902**. Old Town Charlottesville has many one-way streets and limited parking. To reach the Historical Society follow I-64 from Richmond and exit #124 towards Charlottesville (west) onto Route 250. In about 2 miles turn left onto East High Street. In about 1 mile turn right to stay on East High Street. The Society is on 2nd Street, about 6 blocks ahead on your left between Jefferson and Market. If there is no parking available in front of the building, there is a pay-to-park just across Market Street. Enter from 2nd street and self-park. **You must use a credit card** at a small kiosk to pay for parking.
> **(434) 296.7294   albemarlehistory.org**

ORIGINAL DOCUMENTS

Albemarle County Clerk of the Circuit Court has court records that exist from 1632, in the History room of the Courthouse which is entered from the Albemarle County Clerk's Office. There are indices to the early record books.

FIND IT: Court Square, 501 East Jefferson Street, Charlottesville, VA 22902 From the Historical Society exit the side entrance and turn right. Walk up Jefferson Street about 2 blocks. The Courthouse is on your left. As you face the Courthouse, to find the Record Room enter the building annex to the left of the Courthouse. Take the elevator or the stairs to the 2nd floor. The Clerk's Office is down the hall on your right.

GOOD TO KNOW

The University of Virginia is in Charlottesville. The UVA Library Special Collections has a genealogy site that might be helpful before you visit. **genealogy.library.virginia.edu**

If time permits, Jefferson's home at Monticello should not be missed. It is located at 931 Thomas Jefferson Parkway, Charlottesville, VA 2902-7148 **monticello.org** .

There is lots to do and see in and around Charlottesville. (434) 293.6789 **visitcharlottesville.org**

ALLEGHANY COUNTY

Named for the Alleghany Mountains, the county was formed in 1822 from Bath, Botetourt, and Monroe (West Virginia) counties. The county seat is Covington.

 WHERE TO START

FAMILY RESEARCH

There are 3 sites in Covington to find Family History files.
Charles P. Jones Memorial Library has a Virginia Room with access to computers for searching the census and Heritage Quest. You will find maps, and books to aid your research.

> **FIND IT: 406 Riverside St, Covington, VA 24426** Follow I-64 West toward Lexington and exit #14 onto VA-154 towards Covington. Turn left onto Durant Street. Stay on Durant until it becomes Lexington Ave. In ½ mile on Lexington, turn right onto W Riverside Street. The Library is on the left near the intersection with North Maple Ave. **(540) 962.3321**

The Alleghany Highlands Genealogical Society has extensive family files and assistants to help with research.

> **FIND IT: 515 East Pine St, Covington, VA 24426**
> If this is your first stop, exit #16A and keep left onto E Madison Street for about 1 mile. Stay left onto S. Monroe for .5 mi. Turn right onto E Pine Street. **(540) 962.1501**

The Alleghany County Historical Society's mission is to preserve the history of the Alleghany Highlands. Two historic Chesapeake and Ohio Railroad passenger stations are home to the Society.

> **FIND IT: 149 Maple Avenue, Covington, VA 24426**
> The Society is just down Maple Ave from the Library.
> **(540) 965.0149**

ORIGINAL DOCUMENTS

Alleghany County Clerk of the Circuit Court has original documents dating from its founding in 1822. Marriage records date from 1845. The records of Clifton Forge, VA can be found here as well since that Courthouse closed in 2001.

> **FIND IT: 266 West Main Street, Covington, VA, 24426**
> From the library follow W Riverside St. 2 blocks. Turn right on N. Monroe St. The courthouse is one block down. Enter the Courthouse through security. The Record Room is through the first door on the left. **(540) 965.1730**

GOOD TO KNOW

The **Humpback Covered Bridge** is one of the few remaining covered bridges in the United States that was built higher in the middle than on either end; hence the name of "humpback". The bridge was built in 1857 and is also the oldest remaining covered bridge in the state of Virginia. Humpback covered bridge is located 3 miles west of Covington adjacent to U.S. Highway 60 off Rumsey Road (SR 600). Exit # 10 in Virginia off of I-64 is less than 1 mile from the bridge site.

Falling Spring Falls is a breathtaking 80' waterfall that is one of the most visited and photographed spots in the Alleghany Highlands. The scenic waterfall is located on Route 220 in Alleghany County, just five miles north of Covington, Virginia. One of the largest falls in Virginia, it cascades from an overhanging ledge, and is easily visible from the roadway. Hot Springs Rd, Covington, VA 24426. **(540) 962.2178**

AMELIA COUNTY

Amelia County was formed in 1735 from Prince George and Brunswick counties. It was named in honor of Princess Amelia of Great Britain. The county seat is Amelia Court House.

WHERE TO START

FAMILY RESEARCH

The Amelia County Historical Society: The Historical Society has family files, transcribed court records, and old maps to help the researcher. It is open on Monday, and Wednesday from 12 to 4 pm and on Friday from 10 to 2 pm.

> **FIND IT: 16501 Church St., Amelia Court House, VA 23002**. The building is across Church Street from the back of the Courthouse building. Follow US 360 out of Richmond about 20 miles. Turn right onto US Hwy 360 Bus. (Goodes Bridge Road). Turn left onto Virginia Street, and take the second right onto Church Street. The Society is at the end of this street. **(804)561.4559**

ORIGINAL DOCUMENTS

Amelia County Clerk of the Circuit Court has original documents dating from its founding in 1735. The Clerk's Office and Record Room are in the Courthouse building just across Church Street from the Historical Society. This is an excellent place for research. The indices are most helpful. They are by surname and in chronological order. Copies can be made for 50 cents a page. Cameras are allowed.

> **FIND IT: 16441 Court St., Amelia Court House, 23002** Enter the Courthouse from Court Street or from Church Street. The Clerk's Office is on the main floor. **(804) 561.2128**

GOOD TO KNOW

Sailor's Creek State Park is about 8 miles southwest on US 360 in Jetersville, VA. There is a visitor's center and gift shop and easy hiking trails.

Confederate Overlook Trail
The Confederate Overlook Trail is about a 1 mile easy hiking trail that takes you along various points of interest. Interpretive markers can be found along your travels that explain the history of this hallowed ground. Your hike will eventually lead you along Little Sailors Creek and loop back to the start of the trail.

Monument Trail
The Monument Trail is a short, easy trail that takes you to a United States Civil War Memorial for those who fought for both armies at Sailor's Creek and was dedicated in April 2000.

AMHERST COUNTY

Amherst County was formed in 1761 from Albemarle County. It was named for Jeffery Amherst, the Crown Governor of Virginia from 1759 to 1768. The county seat is the town of Amherst.

 **WHERE TO START**

FAMILY RESEARCH

Amherst County Museum & Historical Society:
The Museum has a family history library as well as exhibits about early Amherst County. It includes family files, compiled family history binders, maps, census records and other reference materials.

> **FIND IT: 154 South Main St., Amherst, VA 24521**
> From Richmond make your way south to Route 60 W. Follow VA-60 all the way to the town of Amherst. The "Traffic Circle" is a significant landmark in Amherst as is the single traffic light. From east or west enter the traffic circle and go south on Business 29. This is South Main Street. The Museum is just ahead on the right. A two-story brick house, it sits up on a hill and away from the road. Ample parking is available in the back of the building. **(434) 946.9068   amherstcountymuseum.org**

Amherst County Public Library has reference materials for
genealogy such as indexes to wills, deeds, and marriages. The County Heritage Books which contain histories of the early Amherst County families are available for research as well.

> **FIND IT: 382 S. Main Street, Amherst, VA 24521.** The library is further along S. Main Street from the Museum. Go through the traffic light at Second Street. The Library is on the right, just past the intersection of Kenmore Road and Sunset Drive. **(434) 946.9488   acpl.us**

ORIGINAL DOCUMENTS

Amherst County Clerk of the Circuit Court has original documents dating from its founding in 1761. The Clerk's Office and Record Room are in the Courthouse building.

> **FIND IT: 113 Taylor St., Amherst, VA 24521,** From the Museum continue on South Main Street away from the traffic circle. Turn left onto Second Street and left again onto Taylor Street. Taylor is a very small street. The Courthouse is at the top of the hill. Enter through security. Cell phones are allowed on vibrate and some documents can be photographed.
> **(434) 946.9321**

GOOD TO KNOW

Bear Mountain in Amherst County has been the home of the Monacan people for more than 10,000 years. The **Monacan Indian Museum** includes an Indian Mission Church and an original log cabin school house used by the tribe until the 1960s.
2009 Kenmore Road, Amherst, VA 24521
(434) 946.5391 monocannation.com

The Sweet Briar Museum at **Sweet Briar College**, contains an excellent teaching collection of 18th-, 19th-, and 20th-century American decorative arts. Sweet Briar House and the museum's collections take you back to Central Virginia's plantation era, showcase the 19th-century decorative arts, and capture more than 100 years of College life. Admission is free. **134 Chapel Road, Sweet Briar, VA 24521**
(800) 381.6001 sbc.edu

APPOMATTOX COUNTY

Appomattox is an alternate spelling of Appomattoc , the name of a local group of Powhatan Indians in Virginia. Appomattox County was formed in 1845 from Buckingham, Prince Edward, Charlotte, and Campbell Counties. The county seat is Appomattox.

WHERE TO START

FAMILY RESEARCH

JAMERSON LIBRARY: The library has a genealogy/family history section which is a good place to begin. There are resources about other counties and families there as well.

> **FIND IT: 157 Main Street, Appomattox, VA 24522.** US- 460 W and US 60 W are both good routes to follow into the town of Appomattox, VA. The library is in the center of the Village across from Coleman and Sons, Southern States store. Lots of parking is available next to the library building. **(434) 352.5340**

ORIGINAL DOCUMENTS

Appomattox County Clerk of the Circuit Court Office and Record Room are in the Courthouse building. County Court records were destroyed by fire in 1892. Their records begin after that time.

> **FIND IT: 297 North Court Street, Suite B, Appomattox, VA 24522** From the Library, you must go around the block since Main Street is one way. Continue down Main, turn right on Church, right on Linden and right on Court Street. There is a large parking lot on the south side of the Courthouse Complex. From the parking lot follow the wide sidewalk into the complex. The Clerk's Office and Record Room are in the building on your left. Enter through security. **(434) 352.5275**

GOOD TO KNOW

It is the site of the last battle for the Army of Northern Virginia (CSA) and of Robert E. Lee's surrender to U. S. Grant.

Appomattox Court House National Historical Park: The surrender of Lee took place at the McLean House, now a national historical park. The Visitor Center is in the reconstructed courthouse building on VA Rte 24. **(434) 352.8987 x 26 tourappomattox.com**

Clover Hill Village is a six acre living history village where the heritage of Appomattox comes to life.
(434)352.8024 tourappomattox.com

Appomattox County Historical Museum is in the old Appomattox jail building on Court Street. The architecturally unique structure, built in 1897, contains interesting memorabilia from the Appomattox area.
(434) 352.3910 tourappomattox.com

Appomattox Visitor Information Center, 214 Main Street, Appomattox, VA 24522. Right in the middle of town, the Visitor Information Center features a theater, quaint gift shop, reservations center and more. The Historical Society has items and books for sale in the gift shop. **(434) 352.8999**

ARLINGTON COUNTY

Arlington County was formed in 1789 as Alexandria County and from a part of Fairfax County. It was ceded to the U.S. government in 1789 but was returned to Virginia in 1846. It was renamed to Arlington Co in 1920. The county was named for Henry Bennet, 1st Earl of Arlington. The county seat is Arlington.

 **WHERE TO START**

FAMILY RESEARCH

The Center for Local History at Arlington Public Library has some of the collection kept at a repository off-site. It is a good idea to phone or email ahead to assure that the material you wish to use will be available when you arrive.

> **FIND IT: The Virginia Room, 1015 N Quincy Street, Arlington, VA 22201** From Richmond follow I-95 N and keep right onto I-395 N. In about 9 miles exit #8A onto S Washington Blvd toward Columbia Pike. Travel about 2.5 miles then turn left onto N Lincoln Street which will become Monroe Street. Take the 2nd right onto 10th Street N. There is ample library along 10th Street after crossing Nelson Street. The Library entrance is around the corner to the right on Quincy Street. The Research Room is on the first floor. **(703) 228.5966**

ORIGINAL DOCUMENTS

Arlington County Clerk of Circuit Court serves as custodian of all county court records. Because of the division from then Alexandria County, some record books remain at the Alexandria City Courthouse. However all of the extant Deeds and Wills are available here in Arlington. Original Wills from 1805 to the present are available in Arlington.

FIND IT: Arlington County Circuit Court, 1425 N. Courthouse Rd, Suite 6700, Arlington, VA 22201 From the Library parking lot turn right, back onto 10th Street and then turn right onto Quincy Street and then right onto Washington Blvd. In about ½ mile get in the left lane to enter a large intersection and keep left onto Clarendon Blvd, a divided highway. There is a concrete triangle separating Clarendon and Wilson Blvd. In about .7 mile watch for 15th Street and turn right. Parking for the Courthouse is immediately on your left. Pay for parking at any kiosk with cash or credit and put the receipt on your dashboard. Use the walkway from the center of the lot to cross Courthouse Road, go up the concrete stairs, and enter the Circuit Court building on your right, under the awning. Go through security and take the elevator to the 6th floor. The record room is in suite 6300. The deputy clerks are very helpful. **(703) 228.7010**

GOOD TO KNOW

Arlington County is the site for the famous **Arlington National Cemetery**, established as an American military cemetery during the Civil War. President John F. Kennedy's grave is there, too, marked with the Eternal Flame. Other monuments include **The Tomb of the Unknowns and the Iwo Jima Memorial**. **(703) 607.8000.**

City of Alexandria Library Special Collections, 717 Queen Street, Alexandria, Virginia 22314-2420. Special Collections has many resources to help the genealogist research his or her family's history. The collection focuses mainly on material relating to Alexandria and Virginia in general, but other genealogy resources are available as well. **(703) 746.1720 alexandria.lib.va.us**

Theodore Roosevelt Island provides a walk though nature in this small national park. There is a monument to President Roosevelt himself. Technically a part of Washington, D.C., the island is only accessible by a footbridge from Arlington.

AUGUSTA COUNTY

Augusta County was formed in 1738 from part of Orange County. It was named for Princess Augusta of Saxe-Gotha. The county seat is Staunton.

 **WHERE TO START**

FAMILY RESEARCH

The Augusta County Historical Society's collection spans the time period from the first European settlement in Augusta County until the present.

> **FIND IT: 20-22 New Street, Staunton, VA 24402**
> From I-81 (N or S) exit # 222. Go about 2 miles on Richmond Ave. into Staunton. Turn right onto Coalter Street, left onto Johnson Street, and right onto New Street. The Historical Society is located on the 3rd floor of the R.R. Smith Center for History and Art. A parking garage is located across the street from the Center. **(540) 248.4151 augustacountyhs.org**

The Staunton Public Library has a genealogy room with family files, cemetery records, and various indexes to original records from the courthouse.

> **FIND IT: 1 Churchville Ave., Staunton, VA 24401** The library is in an old school building at the corner of Churchville and Augusta Streets. There is a large parking lot in front surrounded by a low rock wall. From the Historical Society continue west on Johnson Street and turn right (north) onto Augusta Street. The library is about .5 mi ahead.
> **(540) 332.3902 staunton.va.us/directory**

ORIGINAL DOCUMENTS

Augusta County Clerk of the Circuit Court has original documents from 1738. The Clerk's Office and Record Room are in the Courthouse building. This record room provides an excellent guide to the rules for usage, and a map to help locate files.

> **FIND IT: 1 East Johnson Street, PO Box 689, Staunton, VA 24402** The Courthouse is in the center of town. From the Historical Society, walk north on New Street ½ block and turn left onto Barrister Row. The Courthouse entrance is one block down on the left. Enter through security. The Record Room is the first door on the left. If you are driving, there is parking on East Johnson Street.

Staunton City Courthouse: 113 E. Beverly St.

GOOD TO KNOW

Woodrow Wilson Presidential Library and Museum, 20 N. Coalter Street, Staunton, VA 24401 is very near the research locations. **(540) 885.0897 woodrowwilson.org**

The American Shakespeare Center, 10 S Market Street in Staunton, has been established as one of America's premier Shakespeare destinations. **(540) 851.1733 americanshakespearecenter.com**

The Augusta County Genealogical Society, 1759 Jefferson Hwy, Fishersville, VA has a small library within the Augusta County Library in Fishersville, VA. **(540) 885.1991**

Frontier Culture Museum, 1290 Richmond Avenue, Staunton, VA 24401 is a living history museum with self-guided tours of colonial farms settled by different cultures of people who migrated here from the Old World. **(540) 332.7850 frontiermuseum.org**

BATH COUNTY

Bath County was created in 1790 from the counties of Augusta, Botetourt and Greenbrier, WV. It was named for the English city of Bath. The county seat is Warm Springs.

 **WHERE TO START**

FAMILY RESEARCH

Bath County Historical Society and Research Library: The library offers manuscript records including 19th century ledger books and employee lists from Warm and Hot Springs hotels; maps, photographs, slave records, books on local and regional history, and many other items of interest to historians and genealogists. The whole of the Society's holdings provide researchers one locale for the study of Greater Bath, which included large portions of the later counties of Alleghany and Highland as well as Pocahontas, WV.

> **FIND IT: 99 Courthouse Hill Road, Warm Springs, VA 24484** From I-64/I-81 exit onto the Virginia By-Way Hwy 39. In about 50 mi. this road will dead end into Sam Snead Hwy, Rte. 220 S. Turn left. In about 1 mile turn right onto Courthouse Hill Road. Go down the hill and watch for it on the right side of the road. Note: *The Historical Society is next door to the Courthouse.*
> **(540) 839.2543   bathcountyhistory.org**

Bath County Public Library, 96 Courthouse Hill Road includes an excellent local history collection. It is across the street from the Historical Society. **(540) 839.7286**

ORIGINAL DOCUMENTS

Bath County Clerk of the Circuit Court has original documents dating from its founding in 1790. The Clerk's Office and Record Room are in the Courthouse building. The Clerk's Office will direct you to the record room. Deeds and Wills are bound into separate books.

> **FIND IT**: **65 Courthouse Road, Warm Springs, VA 24484**
> Follow directions to the Historical Society. Travel in front of the Courthouse and turn right into the lower parking lot. Follow the road around and park up the hill behind the building. Use the back entrance, take the elevator/stairs to the second floor to the Circuit Court Clerk's Office.   **(540) 839.7226**

GOOD TO KNOW

THE HOMESTEAD, 7696 Sam Snead Hwy, Hot Springs, VA 24445 is an historic resort that has welcomed 22 US Presidents. It is known for championship golf courses and the largest hot springs in a Virginia hotel. **(800) 838.1766   thehomestead.com**

Garth Newel Music Center, 403 Garth Newel Lane, Hot Springs, VA 24445 offers chamber music concerts, a restaurant, and rooms available in the historic Manor House.
(540) 839.5018   garthnewel.org

Douthat State Park, 14239 Douthat State Park Road, Millboro, VA 24460 has been named one of the nation's 10 best by Outside Family Vacation Guide. On the National Register of Historic Places it overlaps Bath and Alleghany counties. A 50-acre lake offers swimming, boating and seasonal trout fishing.   **(540) 862.8100**

The Virginia counties of Charlotte, Bath, and Mathews are significant in that none of them have a traffic signal.

BEDFORD COUNTY

Bedford County was created from Lunenburg County in 1753. Part of Albemarle was added in 1754 and another part of Lunenburg was added even later. The county seat is Bedford.

 WHERE TO START

FAMILY RESEARCH

Bedford Museum and Genealogical Library: This large, excellent library and museum offers a wealth of information about Bedford County. Extensive family files, research books, maps and other resources will aid your research. There are volunteers to assist the visitor. Leave plenty of time to see the museum and do research as well.

> **FIND IT: 201 East Main Street, Bedford, VA 24523**
> From Richmond follow US-360 W (Hull Street) for about 43 miles. Bear right onto Holly Farm(s) Rd. In about 10 miles turn slight right onto US-460 W. In 76 miles, take the US-221 N ramp toward Bedford, VA. This will become East Main Street. A dark red brick building just east of the Bedford County Courthouse, the museum faces East Main Street. There is parking on the east side of the building and in the back. An elevator provides easy access to the museum. Find the elevator at the back of the building.
> **(540) 586.4520 bedfordmuseum.org**

ORIGINAL DOCUMENTS

Bedford County Clerk of the Circuit Court has original documents dating from its founding in 1753. The Clerk's Office and Record Room are in the Courthouse building.

FIND IT: 123 East Main Street, Bedford, VA 24523
From the Museum continue up East Main and turn right onto
Court Street. Down the hill there are 2 entrances on the left to
covered parking. The second entrance or lower level is for visitors.
There is additional parking in open lots behind the building.
Find the public elevator near the stairs or walk up to the pavilion.
Enter the building around to your left and through security and
go up to the second floor. The Clerk's Office and Record Room
are well marked. No cameras or cell phones. **(540) 586.7632**

GOOD TO KNOW

The Bedford Visitor Center is located near US 460 and VA 122 at **816
Burks Hill Road, Bedford, VA 24523 National D-Day Memorial
tickets are bought here. www.visitbedford.com**

The National D-Day Memorial, 3 Overlord Circle, Bedford, VA 24523
serves as the national memorial for American veterans who died during
the World War II invasion of Normandy, France on June 6, 1944. It is in
Bedford because the town lost more soldiers per capita than any other town.
(540) 587.3619   dday.org

Thomas Jefferson's private retreat, **Poplar Forest, 1542 Bateman Bridge
Road, Forest, VA 24551** is a National Historic Landmark. It is a not-to-be-
missed destination just north-east of the town of Bedford toward Lynchburg.
poplarforest.org

**Peaks of Otter Lodge, 85554 Blue Ridge Parkway, Bedford, VA
24523** Located at Mile Post 86, the Lodge is a good place to begin
exploring this beautiful region.

BLAND COUNTY

Bland County was formed in 1861 from Wythe, Tazewell, and Giles Counties. More land was added from Giles County after this date. The county was named for Richard Bland, a leader of Colonial Virginia. The county seat is Bland.

 WHERE TO START

FAMILY RESEARCH

Bland County Historical Society: The Historical Society has an extensive genealogy library. The Society web site provides an index to the collection. The Courthouse, Library, and Historical Society are almost next door to each other.

> **FIND IT: 19 Courthouse Street, Bland, VA 24315.** Follow I-64 W to I-81 S and merge onto I-77 at exit 72 towards Bluefield. In about 12 miles exit #52 towards Bland (east) onto U. S. Hwy 52. Follow Hwy 52 into Bland, turn right onto Main Street at the stop sign. The Society is in the old jail building on Courthouse Street. This street is on your right when facing the front of the Courthouse. It runs beside the Courthouse between Main Street and Jackson Street. **(276) 688.0088 blandcountyhistsoc.org**

Bland County Library: The library has a collection of books, microfilm, periodicals, maps, etc. which assist library users in researching the history of Southwest Virginia and surrounding areas. Genealogy databases also provide online access to family information and vital records.

> **FIND IT: 697 Main Street, Bland, VA 24315.** The library is one block from the Historical Society. **(276) 688.3737 sbrl.org**

ORIGINAL DOCUMENTS

Bland County Clerk of the Circuit Court has most of the original documents dating from its founding in 1861. The Courthouse burned in 1888 and some early records were lost. Deeds, wills, and court order books from 1861 are still available. There is a register of marriage bonds but the original bonds are gone.

> **FIND IT: 612 Main Street, Suite 104, Bland, VA 24315**
> Follow the directions for the Historical Society into Bland. Park on the street. Enter the Courthouse through the front entrance on Main Street. The Clerk's Office and Record Room are down the hall on the right. Cameras are allowed but no scanners.
> **(276) 688.4562**

GOOD TO KNOW

The Mountain Home Center is a celebration of rural life in Bland County. Oral history and technology activities of the Bland History Archives are here. Contact jdodson@mac.com to schedule a visit. **blandcountyhistoryarchives.org.**

Sharon Lutheran Church and Cemetery is a historic Lutheran church and cemetery located near Ceres, VA with a collection of rare Germanic gravestones.

Wolf Creek Bridge is an historic metal Pratt truss railroad bridge located near Rocky Gap, VA. The bridge was closed in 1987, and became a pedestrian bridge and the focal point of a county recreational park.

Wolf Creek Indian Village is a museum dedicated to the history of the first Native American people who called the mountains of Bland County home. **indianvillage.org.**

BOTETOURT COUNTY

Botetourt County was formed from Augusta County in 1769 and named for the Baron de Botetourt. Fincastle was founded in 1772 and named for Lord Fincastle, son of Lord Dunmore, Virginia's last royal governor. The county seat is Fincastle.

WHERE TO START

FAMILY RESEARCH

The Fincastle Library: A special room in this library is dedicated to genealogical research. Books and files of family histories, cemetery information, books on other counties in Virginia and on Virginia history are available to the researcher.

> **FIND IT: 11 Academy Street, Fincastle, VA 24090** Exit 162 from I-64/I-81 S toward Buchanan onto US 11. In about 3 miles turn slight right onto Blue Ridge Parkway. In about 5 miles the Parkway becomes E. Main Street. Keep left, go .2 mi and turn left onto S Church Street. Take the 2nd right onto Academy Street. Library is ahead on the left. Lots of parking. **(540) 473.8339**

The Botetourt Historical Society: The Botetourt County Historical Society maintains the Botetourt County History Museum, located behind the Courthouse in Fincastle.

> **FIND IT: 1 West Main Street.** From the library continue on Academy Street and turn right onto S. Roanoke Street. Go two blocks and turn left onto East Main Street. The museum is to the left and behind the Courthouse. Limited parking at the Courthouse. (540) 473.8394

ORIGINAL DOCUMENTS

Botetourt County Clerk of the Circuit Court has most of the original documents dating from its founding in 1769. An excellent guide to genealogical resources in this county can be found through a series of links from the Botetourt County web site. **co.botetourt.va.us/libraries.** In the **Jump links** menu choose *genealogy resources.* Under the **Clerk's Office** choose **records available.** There is also a map of the record room which shows the location of these resources. Much of your research will be self- guided unless there is a volunteer from the library there on that day.

> **FIND IT: 1 W Main Street, Fincastle, VA 24090-0219**
> Follow directions for the History Museum. The Circuit Court Clerk's Office is the far right door of the Courthouse as you face the building. **(540) 473.8274**

GOOD TO KNOW

More than a dozen Botetourt sites are on the Virginia Historic Landmarks Register. **Breckinridge Mill, Callie Furnace, Nininger's Mill (Tinker Mill), Phoenix Bridge, Prospect Hill, Roaring Run Furnace at Roaring Run, Santillane, Wiloma, Wilson Warehouse** in Buchanan and **archaeological sites at Bessemer** near Eagle Rock and at **Looney Mill Creek** near Buchanan.

Locks, canal abutments and tunnels from the James River and Kanawha Canal offer a look at the country's early mode of transportation.

In the town of Buchanan, the only swinging bridge that crosses the James River is on abutments that date back 150 years.

A marker in Fincastle notes that Meriwether Lewis and William Clark departed from this frontier town when they were commissioned by President Thomas Jefferson to explore the Louisiana Purchase. Other markers point to frontier forts and sites of Indian raids.

BRUNSWICK COUNTY

Brunswick County was first formed in 1720 from Prince George County. In 1732 more land was added from parts of Surry and Isle of Wight counties. In 1745 a series of new counties was formed and the current western border established. In 1780 Greensville County was formed from part of Brunswick's eastern side. The county is named for the former Duchy of Brunswick-Lunenburg in Germany. The county seat is Lawrenceville.

 WHERE TO START

FAMILY RESEARCH

Brunswick County Library: A part of the Meherrin Regional Library System, this library maintains a history room with many resources for genealogy.

> **FIND IT: 133 Hicks St, Lawrenceville, VA 23868**
> From Richmond drive south on I-95 about 23 miles to exit 51 and merge onto I-85 S. In about 29 miles exit #30 and turn left onto Rte. 712/Old Stage Road toward Rawlings. In about 12 miles turn right onto US-58. In about 3 miles take US-58Bus on the right. Follow it about 2 miles all the way into Lawrenceville. US-58Bus will end at Hicks Street. Turn right. The Library is ahead on the right. The building sits facing directly onto Hicks Street. There is 2 hour parking in front. **(434) 848.2418   meherrinlib.org**

ORIGINAL DOCUMENTS

Brunswick County Clerk of the Circuit Court has most of the original records from 1732.

FIND IT: 216 N. Main Street, Lawrenceville, VA 23868 From the Library go back up Hicks Street and turn to go in front of the Court Complex. The first building on the right is the County Museum. The middle building is the Circuit Court Clerk's Office and Record Room. The last building is the new Courthouse. There is 2 hour parking on the street. There is a large parking lot behind the Complex. Just stay straight on Hicks Street and walk back up to Main Street. **(434) 848.2215**

GOOD TO KNOW

Lawrenceville Historic District is roughly bounded by W. Sixth Avenue, Maria Street, Rose Creek and Thomas Street and includes 1829 Saint Andrew's Episcopal Church. It is on the National Register of Historic Places in Virginia.

Site of **Fort Christanna completed in 1714.** The fort was built as a protective place for local Native American tribes to live, trade, and get schooling for their children. Find it just south of town on VA-46 toward Gholsonville, VA.

Roanoke River Rails to Trails, Inc. – Tobacco Heritage Trail
The trail is a recreational outlet for hiking, walking, jogging, biking and horseback riding along abandoned railroad beds. Region one begins in Lawrenceville and continues through South Hill in Mecklenburg County. **tobaccoheritagetrail.org**

County Park at Great Creek is located on the outskirts of Lawrenceville. This public park is on the banks of Great Creek Reservoir, a 212 acre flood control lake. It is open April through October.

BUCHANAN COUNTY

Buchanan County was formed in 1858 from parts of Tazewell County from the east, and Russell County from the south. The county was named for James Buchanan, the 15th president of the United States from 1857-1861. In 1880 the southwestern part of Buchanan County was combined with parts of Russell County and Wise County to become Dickenson County. Buchanan courthouse burned and all of the records before 1885 were destroyed. The county seat is Grundy.

WHERE TO START

FAMILY RESEARCH

Buchanan Public Library: The Buchanan County Public Library should be your first stop. The library has a large genealogy and local family history collection. The Historical Society also has a large data base of family names, and volunteers to help with searches. The Historical Society also meets at the Library in Grundy, VA. It does not have a separate location for research.

> **FIND IT: 1185 Poe Town Road, Grundy, VA 24614.** From I-81 exit 72 onto I-77 toward Bluefield and Charleston W.VA. Take exit 1 down and around to head back east on Hwy 52. In about 3 miles this will merge into Hwy 460 W. Follow 460/Riverside Drive through Bluefield, VA for about 72 miles. Just past an intersection with Edgewater Drive, watch for a right turn up and onto Poe Town Road. The Library is ahead on the right. **(276) 935.5721   bcplnet.org**

ORIGINAL DOCUMENTS

Buchanan County Clerk of the Circuit Court has most of the original documents dating from its founding in 1858. The Clerk's Office and Record Room are in the Courthouse building.

FIND IT: **1012 Walnut Street, Suite 210, Grundy, VA 24614.** Follow directions to the Library except turn right onto Edgewater/ VA 83 E before you reach Poe Town Street. Take the first right onto Main Street. The Courthouse is at the corner of Main and Walnut. The building is well marked. Use the entrance to the left of the arches. Go to the Clerk's office on the second floor and ask for the Records Room. **(276) 935.6567**

GOOD TO KNOW

Buchanan County is known by the locals as Buck-anan. It was the heart of coal mining country in Virginia. **bucanancountyinfo.org**

The Mike Young Trail is a three-mile long biking/walking trail located on Slate Creek Road, State Route 83 that starts near the hospital in Grundy.

The Bull Creek Trail is a three-mile long biking/walking trail located on Bull Creek Road, State Route 609 at Harman.

The Coal Heritage Trail which begins in Tazewell County meanders throughout Buchanan County.

The Breaks Interstate Park is adjacent to the Buchanan County Line. This park has been called the "Grand Canyon of the South". **www.breakspark.com**

"Round the Mountain" trail sites can be found near and in Grundy, VA. The Artisan Trails of Southwest Virginia highlights places to find home grown and handmade items.

BUCKINGHAM COUNTY

Buckingham County was formed in 1761 from the southeastern portion of Albemarle County. This is the only Buckingham County in the entire United States. It was probably named for the Duke of Buckingham. The county seat is Buckingham Court House.

 WHERE TO START

FAMILY RESEARCH

The Housewright House: Historic Buckingham, Inc. serves as the headquarters for the Historical Society, as well as a museum and a repository for historical books, genealogical records and other resources, such as cemetery surveys and maps. They also have a family file index. The Museum is open April through November, or call for an appointment.

> **FIND IT: 13012 West James Anderson Hwy, Buckingham Court House, VA 23921.** From Richmond, follow Hwy 60 W straight into Buckingham Court House. The building is a brick home directly across the street from the parking lot for the Buckingham County Courthouse building.
> **(434) 969.4304 historicbuckingham.org**

The local library in Dillwyn, VA has a local history section that might help with family research.

> **FIND IT: 1140 Main Street, Dillwyn, VA 23936.** From the Courthouse follow Hwy 60 East to Sprouses Corner and turn left onto US-15 N. The library is about 3 miles ahead on the right.
> **(434) 983.3848 buckinghamlibrary.org**

ORIGINAL DOCUMENTS

Buckingham County Clerk of the Circuit Court has few of the original records because a fire destroyed the Jefferson Court House in 1869. The original records from 1869 are here in the record room. The Grantor and Grantee **Index** to Deeds dates from 1762 – 1909.

> **FIND IT: 13061 West James Anderson Hwy, Buckingham Court House, VA 23921.** Follow directions for the Historical Society. Parking is on the west side of the building. Walk around and follow the signs to the Clerk's office on the east side of the building. **(434) 969.4984**

GOOD TO KNOW

Buckingham County is the geographic center of the state. There is a living history village called **The Village at Lee Wayside, 84 Lee Way Road, Buckingham, VA 23931**, which is open on Saturdays and Sundays April - November. The historic property of Rose Cottage was a stagecoach stop and it is the spot where General Robert E. Lee camped on his way back to Richmond two days after his surrender at Appomattox. **leewaysidevillage.com**

Historic Buckingham shares operation of **Hatton Ferry, 10120 Hatton Ferry Road, Scottsville, VA.** It is a cable ferry located 5.5 miles west of Scottsville, Virginia on the James River. It is the last poled ferry in the United States. The ferry crosses the river upstream of Scottsville between Albemarle County and Buckingham County. A seasonal service, the Hatton Ferry operates on a weekend schedule from April to October. **thehattonferry.org**

CAMPBELL COUNTY

Campbell County was formed in 1782 from Bedford County. Some parts of the county were taken away and added to Appomattox County at a later time. The county was named for Revolutionary War hero, General William Campbell, who is known for the 1780 Battle of Kings Mountain. The county seat is Rustburg.

WHERE TO START

FAMILY RESEARCH

Campbell County Public Library: The Virginia Room of this library provides a wonderful collection of research materials for Campbell County as well as outlying counties and the City of Lynchburg. The Room is on the lower level. Ask for the brochure which provides a guide to the resources in the Virginia Room.

> **FIND IT: 684 Village Hwy, Rustburg, VA 24588.** From Richmond follow US-360 W (Hull Street) for about 43 miles. Bear right onto Holly Farm(s) Rd. In about 10 miles turn slight right onto US-460 W. In 44 miles, turn left onto VA-24/Village Hwy. This is the road into Rustburg. In about 10 miles the Library is just past Courthouse Lane on the right. There is a large parking lot for the Library and the Courthouse Complex. **(434) 332.9560   campbellcountylibraries.org**

The Campbell County Historical Society and Museum:
The Museum is housed in the old historic Courthouse.
It is currently open only by appointment.
(434) 821.1681   campbellcountyvahistoricalsociety.org

ORIGINAL DOCUMENTS

Campbell County Clerk of the Circuit Court has most of the original documents dating from its founding in 1782. The Clerk's Office and Record Room are in the Courthouse building.

> **FIND IT:** Follow the directions to the County Library. The Courthouse and the Library face a common parking lot, one on each side. Enter the Courthouse through security and turn left around the corner to reach the Clerk's Office.
> **(434) 332.9500 x3 x1**

GOOD TO KNOW

Rustburg – was established as the county seat in 1784 when Jeremiah Rust donated land for the first court house. Numerous old buildings line the streets of this village, including the 1848 Court House, now listed on the National Register of Historic Places. Also in Rustburg is Nickup, formerly a tavern where Patrick Henry rested on trips between his homes.
Home of Anne Spencer: The home of Harlem Renaissance poet Anne Spencer is located at 1313 Pierce Street, Lynchburg, Virginia just north of Campbell County. Tours by appointment only. **(434) 847.1459**

Jones Memorial Library: 23110 Memorial Ave., Lynchburg, VA. The Library is a genealogical treasure chest of references. You will find family histories, cemetery records, county records, military records just to name a few. **(804) 846.0522**

The Willie Hodges Booth Museum, 205 Lynchburg Ave, Brookneal, VA. 24528 The Museum is located within the Patrick Henry Memorial Library, a branch of the Campbell County Public Library System. It contains a Virginia Collection as well as displays and artifacts about Brookneal's history and families, from its roots in tobacco and manufacturing to local son, General Pick, of WWII Burma Road fame. **(434) 376.3363**

CAROLINE COUNTY

Caroline County was formed from Essex, King and Queen and King William Counties in 1728. It was named for Queen Caroline of Brandenburg-Ansbach, wife of King George II of Great Britain. The county seat is Bowling Green.

 ## WHERE TO START

FAMILY RESEARCH

Caroline County Library: There are a number of transcriptions of abstracts of Caroline County records that should be studied before beginning a search among the original records. This the best place to begin. There is a basic genealogy room and the Herbert Collins Room which requires an appointment to use.

> **FIND IT: 17202 Richmond Tpke, Milford, VA 22514** Drive north on I-95 about 30 miles to exit #104 and keep right to merge onto VA-207 toward Bowling Green. Continue on this road about 4 miles to merge with US-301. Turn right (south) on US-301. The library is in the Caroline County Community Services Center ahead on the right. It is across from a service station. Turn into the parking lot and enter through the front. **(804) 633.5455   carolinelibrary.org**

ORIGINAL DOCUMENTS

Caroline County Clerk of the Circuit Court suffered loss of many of the early records of Caroline County during the American Civil War.

> **FIND IT: 112 Courthouse Lane, Suite A, Bowling Green, VA 22427.** From the library head north (make a U-turn) on US-301. In about 2 miles turn right onto Courthouse Lane.

The Clerk's Office is ahead on the right. Park on the street or turn onto Butler Street and park in the back of the Courthouse. **(804) 633.5800**

GOOD TO KNOW

Central Rappahannock Heritage Center, 900 Barton St. #111, Fredericksburg, VA 22401 The Central Rappahannock Heritage Center has historical documents and photographs pertaining to the history and people from the counties of Caroline, Stafford, King George, Spotsylvania and the City of Fredericksburg in Virginia. **(540) 373.3704   crhcarchives.org**

Caroline County is home to **The Meadow stables**, the birthplace of **the** renowned racehorse **Secretariat**, winner of the 1973 Kentucky Derby, Preakness Stakes and Belmont Stakes: The Triple Crown. **Caroline County Visitor Center 23724 Rogers Clark Boulevard, Ruther Glen, VA 22546**

The Caroline County Visitor Center's **whale display** is a resin cast of the skeleton of a 14 million year old new species, of Eobalaenoptera found in Caroline County. The Visitor Center mounting is considered one of the most innovative paleontological whale displays in the world. **(804) 633.3490   visitcaroline.com**

Port Royal, VA is one of the area's more historic towns. John Wilkes Booth was shot and killed here. **The Museum of American History** at 506 Main Street is in Port Royal. **(804) 742.5406**

Drive along the historic **American Revolution Washington-Rochambeau Route** of September 1781 as you enter and leave Caroline County.

CARROLL COUNTY

Carroll County was formed in 1842 from Grayson County. The county is named for Charles Carroll, a signer of the Declaration of Independence, from Maryland. Part of Patrick County was added later. The county seat is Hillsville.

WHERE TO START

FAMILY RESEARCH

The Carroll County Historical Society and Museum:
This is the best place to begin. Inside the Old Courthouse, the Society maintains one of the largest, private genealogy databases in the state. The information in their database is currently at more than 213,000 Carroll-connected people. They have marriage records, death records, census records, and family histories as well.

> **FIND IT: 515 N Main Street, Hillsville, VA 24343**
> Follow I-64W to I-81 south and exit #81 onto I-77S. In about 20 miles at exit 14, turn left onto US-58N into Hillsville. In .2 mile turn left at traffic light onto US-58E/Carrollton Pike. In 2.5 miles turn left onto N Main Street. The old courthouse is ahead on the right. Park on the street.
> **(276) 728.4113   historicalsociety.chillsnet.org**

ORIGINAL DOCUMENTS

Carroll County Clerk of the Circuit Court has most of the original documents dating from its founding in 1842. The Clerk's Office and Record Room are in the Courts and Administration building.

> **FIND IT: 605 Pine Street, Hillsville, VA 24343**
> From the Society, in .3 miles turn right onto Court Street and in about 100 yards turn left onto Pine Street. The Courts building is

ahead on the right. Good parking in front. Go through security and then up to the second floor. The Deed Room is around the corner from the elevator.

GOOD TO KNOW:

Take a walking tour of **Historic Hillsville** to see the historic courthouse, museum, genealogy information center, library, new county complex, the Beaver Dam Walking Trail, Wellness Center, and the Carter Pines Park and trail links.

There are natural wonders in Carroll County that include **The Blue Ridge Parkway** which crosses the entire southern part of the county. Wonderful views and quiet scenic stops, lots of trails and supporting features can be found here.

The Devil's Den is a unique private nature preserve located just off the Blue Ridge Parkway on a crest of the Blue Ridge Escarpment. Devil's Den refers to a 600-million-year-old cave formation on the side of mountain. This type of cavern is unique in that it was formed by the movement of rock. The Preserve is open sunrise-sunset, May-November. 80 Cemetery Road, **Fancy Gap**, VA 24328. **(276) 730.3100**

The Blue Ridge Music Center 700 Foothills Rd. Galax, VA 24333. The Center is being linked to a mountain music trail called **The Crooked Road**. The Center is located off the Blue Ridge Parkway and provides ready access to the Pipers Gap, Fancy Gap and Galax areas. The general area is often called the birthplace and soul of old time and bluegrass music. **(276) 236.5309**

CHARLES CITY COUNTY

Charles City was one of four boroughs or incorporations created by instructions of the London Company delivered to Jamestown in 1618. Seventeen additional counties and eight independent cities were formed out of its original boundaries. The county seat is Charles City.

 ## WHERE TO START

FAMILY RESEARCH

Charles City County Richard M. Bowman Center for Local History, is a county-owned reference library and archives. The collection includes extensive resources pertaining to Charles City and the surrounding region. Microfilm of early records can be found here as well.

> **FIND IT: 10600 Courthouse Road, Charles City, VA 23030**
> The most direct route out of Richmond is East Main Street/ VA-5/US-60. In about 13 miles turn right onto VA-106/609 S. In about 1 mile turn left to stay on VA-609 S. In about 4 miles keep left to stay on Rte. 602. In about 6 miles turn right onto VA-155 S. In about 1 ½ miles cross Hwy 5 onto Rte 644, Courthouse Road. The library is the first building ahead on the left. There is plenty of parking in the front.
> **(804) 652.1516   charlescity.org/genealogical-databases**

ORIGINAL DOCUMENTS

Charles City County Clerk of the Circuit Court has undergone heavy record loss. Some deed books, will books, minute books, and order books from 1789 to present still exist. There are 5 order books from the 1600s.

FIND IT: 10780 Courthouse Road, Charles City, VA 23030-0086 From the History Center continue on Courthouse Road to the next driveway on the left. Enter the Courthouse through the arches. The record room is on the first floor. **(804) 652.2105**

GOOD TO KNOW

Charles City County features some of the larger and older of the extant James River plantations along State Route 5. All are privately owned. Many of the houses and/or grounds are open daily to visitors with various admission fees applicable. Some James River plantations open to the public, include:

Berkeley Plantation, 12602 Harrison Landing Rd
(804) 829.6018

Edgewood Plantation, 4800 John Tyler Memorial Highway
(804) 829.2962

Kittiewan Plantation, 12104 Weyanoke Road
(804) 829.2272

North Bend Plantation, 12200 Weyanoke Road
(804) 829.5176

Sherwood Forest Plantation, 14501 John Tyler Highway
(804) 829.5377

Shirley Plantation, 501 Shirley Plantation Road
(804) 829.5121

Westover Plantation, 7000 Westover Road
(804) 829.2882

CHARLOTTE COUNTY

Charlotte County was formed from Lunenburg County in 1764. It is named for Queen Charlotte, wife of King George III. The Virginia counties of Charlotte, Bath, and Matthews are significant in that none of them have a traffic signal. The county seat is Charlotte Court House.

 ## WHERE TO START

FAMILY RESEARCH

Charlotte County Public Library: Family Histories, County Reference books, and other genealogy resources can be found here. It is the best place to begin. Many of the resources are available on their web site.

> **FIND IT: 112 LeGrande Ave., Charlotte Court House, VA 23923.** Out of Richmond follow I-95S, or US-360/Hull Street, or Powhite Parkway out of town to merge onto VA-288S and then onto US-360W toward Amelia. In about 75 total miles take the US-360Bus W exit toward Farmville. This road becomes Four Locust Hwy. In about 2 miles turn right onto US-40/Church Street. This becomes George Washington Hwy. In about 9 miles turn left onto David Bruce Ave. Go in front of the Courthouse and turn left onto Legrande Ave. Library is second building down on the right. Park on the street.
> **(434) 542.5247   cclibrary.net**

Charlotte County Historical and Genealogical Society, **600 David Bruce Ave. Charlotte C.H., VA 23923.** The Society is open Wednesdays and the 1st and 3rd Saturdays from 1-5 PM. There are research files available.

ORIGINAL DOCUMENTS

Charlotte County Clerk of the Circuit Court has most of the original documents dating from its founding in 1764. The Clerk's Office and Record Room are in the Courthouse building. Some marriage records are missing.

> **FIND IT: 125 David Bruce Avenue, Charlotte CH, VA 23923**
> Follow the directions to the Library. Walk across LeGrande and along in front of the Court House on the brick sidewalk. The Clerk's Office is in the building that sits parallel to the Courthouse facing David Bruce Ave. When you pass the cannon, turn right down the driveway. Use the side entrance from here. The front entrance isn't used very much. If you decide to drive, there is parking down this driveway in the back of the building.

GOOD TO KNOW

For more than one hundred years **the Clarkton Bridge** has spanned the 250 feet wide Staunton River connecting the counties of Halifax and Charlotte. The bridge stands 53' over the riverbed.
The iron beams were assembled on site into a bridge design known as a camelback truss. It is a magnificent through-truss bridge with a long entrance ramp on the Charlotte County entrance. The entrance on the Halifax County side is on a winding road along a cliff.
virginia.org/historicsites/clarktonbridge

The Museum and Visitors Center of Charlotte County in the Old Jail on Courthouse Square should not be missed. Download the walking tour map of the Court House from their web site.
charlotteva.com/museum

CHESTERFIELD COUNTY

Chesterfield County was formed in 1749 from Henrico County. The James River is the dividing line between the two counties. The county seat is Chesterfield.

 **WHERE TO START**

This County is fortunate to have an active Historical Society as well as a large Local History Room in the Central library. Call the Historical Society or the Library to arrange an appointment if you need research assistance.

FAMILY RESEARCH

Chesterfield County Public Library

> **FIND IT: 9501 Lori Frith Road, Chesterfield, VA 23832**.
> The library is near the courthouse complex. From Route 288, exit onto Iron Bridge Road east toward Chesterfield. Turn left at the second traffic light onto Lucy Corr Boulevard. The entrance is on the right. **(804)748.1603   library.chesterfield.gov**

Chesterfield County Historical Society

> **FIND IT: 10201 Iron Bridge Road, Chesterfield, VA 23832**
> From I-95 S Exit #61 and turn right onto VA-613/Willis Rd. It will end at US-1. Turn left and then take the next right onto Kingsdale Road. In about 1 mile turn left onto Chester Rd. In 1 mile turn right onto VA-145W /Centralia Road. In about 3 miles turn right onto Iron Bridge Road. The Historical Society is ahead on the right. Watch for the large sign. **From the Library** go back to Iron Bridge Road and turn left. Go about 1.5 miles, make a legal U-turn. The Society is ahead on the right.
> **(804) 796.7121**

ORIGINAL DOCUMENTS

Chesterfield County Clerk of the Circuit Court has most of the original documents dating from its founding in 1749. All of the early deed books, will books, and order books have been microfilmed. The original books are not available for viewing. The indices to wills and deeds are still available in the original bound volumes. The Record room has many computers which are also used by persons doing title and land searches. Obtain a copy card at the front desk and ask for instructions on using the computers. Be aware, not all of the computers have printers attached. Copies are 50 cents per page.

> **FIND IT: 9500 Courthouse Road, Chesterfield, VA 23832**
> The Courthouse Complex is very near the Central Library. Everyone must enter the Courthouse Complex through a metal detector. You are not allowed to bring in cameras or tape recorders or cell phones. Ask for the Record Room and the guards will direct you.   **(804) 748.1241**

GOOD TO KNOW

Henricus Historical Park is an outdoor living-history museum where visitors interact through "hands-on" encounters with period-dressed historical interpreters of the English settlers and Virginia Indians. The site includes more than a dozen recreated colonial structures where visitors can learn about, and participate in, cooking, blacksmithing, militia drills, planting and harvesting. It is closed on Mondays.
(804) 748.1613   henricus.org

Pamplin Historical Park and The National Museum of the Civil War Soldier is a National Historic Landmark. Pamplin Historical Park is recognized as one of America's premier historical attractions and as the most innovative Civil War history park in the country.
(804) 861.2408   pamplinpark.org

CLARKE COUNTY

Clarke County, named for Revolutionary War hero, General George Rogers Clark, was formed in 1836 from Frederick County. The county seat is Berryville.

 **WHERE TO START**

FAMILY RESEARCH

Clarke County Historical Association Museum tells the story of Clarke County and her many unique and historic families. Exhibits in each room cover a different time period. The second floor is dedicated to research and preservation. The extensive archive collection is available on-line and on-site research assistance is offered as well.

> **FIND IT: 32 East Main Street, Berryville, VA 22611.**
> From Richmond, make your way to I-66W. Exit #23 onto US-17N/US-50. In about 8 miles turn left onto US-50W (Mosby Highway). In about 5 miles turn right onto Millwood Road. In about 2 miles turn right onto VA-255, Bishop Meade Road. (Watch carefully for this turn). In about 3 more miles turn left to stay on Bishop Meade Rd. It will dead end into 340 N, turn right. Go 3 more miles and turn right onto East Main Street. The Museum is down on the left. Park in the rear or on the street. **(540) 955.2600 clarkehistory.org**

ORIGINAL DOCUMENTS

Clarke County Clerk of the Circuit Court has most of the original documents dating from its founding in 1836. The Clerk's Office and Record Room are in the Courthouse building.

FIND IT: 104 N Church St, Berryville, VA 22611
The Courthouse and Record Room are walking distance from
the Museum. Walk back to Church Street and turn right. The
new 1960s courthouse is ahead on the right. Enter between the
columns and through the front door. The Record Room is down
this main hallway on the right. **(540) 955.5116**

GOOD TO KNOW

This area was part of Lord Fairfax's 5 million acre property. Lord Fairfax
built his American home at what is now the village of White Post, named
for the large signpost pointing the way to Lord Fairfax's office. During the
Civil War, John Singleton Mosby, "the Gray Ghost" of the Confederacy,
criss-crossed the county. General Robert E. Lee, whose wife was born in
Clarke County, camped here on his way to Gettysburg. There is a park
and small playground across the street from the Museum. Ask at the
Museum for a map of the walking tour of Berryville.

The stone "Old Chapel" is **the oldest Episcopal Church** building
still in continuous use west of the Blue Ridge Mountains. The original
construction was of logs circa 1738. The Chapel is located at the
intersection of Route 340 and Route 255 and has a cemetery on
the grounds.

**The State Arboretum of Virginia, 400 Blandy Farm Lane, Boyce, VA
22620** includes 175 acres with more than 8,000 trees and woody shrubs.
The grounds are open to the public with both walking and driving loops
within this remarkable park-like setting. Facilities include a 10-room
brick slave quarters built between 1825 and 1830.
(540) 837.1758   clarkecounty.gov/tourism

Clarke African American Cultural Center
(540) 955.5512   jschoolmuseum.org

CRAIG COUNTY

Craig County was formed from Botetourt, Roanoke, Giles, and Monroe (in present-day West Virginia) Counties in 1851. It was named for Robert Craig, a 19th-century Virginia congressman. The county seat is New Castle.

 ## WHERE TO START

FAMILY RESEARCH

The Craig County Historical Society and Museum:
The Historical Society maintains a genealogy library in the Old Brick Hotel across the street from the Craig County Courthouse. It is open most Fridays and by appointment.

> **FIND IT:** Exit #141 from I-81 S toward New Castle. Keep left around and turn left onto N Electric Road/VA-419. In about ½ mile turn right onto VA-311/Salem Avenue. In about 19 miles turn left onto Main Street. The Courthouse is ahead on the corner and the Historical Society is across the street.
> **(540) 864.5489**

ORIGINAL DOCUMENTS

Craig County Clerk of the Circuit Court has most of the original documents dating from its founding in 1851. The deputy clerks will help you when they can. The Clerk's Office and Record Room are in the Courthouse building.

> **FIND IT: 303 Main St., New Castle 24127** Follow the directions to the Historical Society. The Courthouse is across the street. Enter from the front, go all the way to the end of the hall, down a few steps and turn right. **(540) 864.6141**

GOOD TO KNOW

New Castle features one of the Commonwealth's antebellum court complexes, including a porticoed courthouse built in 1851.

Fenwick Iron Mines
Remnants of an iron-mining community and iron works from the 1890s-1920s; interpretive wetland and forest trail. Seven miles northeast of New Castle on Rt. 685. Picnic area. (Reserve shelter ahead of time).

Tingler's Mill
Route 311 west to Route 18, Paint Bank, VA 24131
A grist mill built in 1873 and used until 1965. In 2004, the mill pond was revitalized and is now stocked with trout, which you can feed. Recently the entire exterior of the mill was restored, a new race was constructed and the big wheel is once again turning. Restoration of the inside of the building is on-going as the present owners continue to bring the mill back to its former beauty and function. Presently, you may tour the first floor. Currently, there are local crafters selling their wares and holding demonstrations in the mill every weekend from early spring until late fall. **tingler'smill.com**

The **Keffer Log House** was rebuilt during the summer of 1999 by Roger Davis of Montana and Robert Echols of Happy Hollow. Mr. Echols lived next door to the Keffers when he was young. The lot on which this cabin is located was the horse corral used by men coming to Court in New Castle. There is a (fake) outhouse on the property.

The **Hawkins-Brizendine Cabin** was built in 2000 of logs from the funeral home given by Buddy Boitnott and from the Hawkins homeplace on Rt. 614 given by Ashby & Flo Eakin. Cabins can be visited Fridays 1 – 4 PM April – November
(540) 864.5489   craigcountyva.gov/the-cabins

CULPEPER COUNTY

Culpeper County was formed in 1749 from Orange County. The county is named for Thomas Culpeper, an early Virginia governor. In July 1749, 17-year-old George Washington was commissioned as the first County surveyor. The county seat is Culpeper.

 WHERE TO START

FAMILY RESEARCH

Culpeper County Library Local History Room: This is the best place to begin. The researcher will find family history books and vertical files of family genealogies. There are maps, county resource books, and access to genealogy web sites. There is usually someone there to help guide your research.

> **FIND IT: 271 Southgate Shopping Center, Culpeper, VA 22701.** From Richmond follow I-95 North about 55 miles to exit 130B toward Culpeper. Merge onto VA-3W. In about 30 miles this will become Fredericksburg Hwy. Straight ahead through two traffic lights, turn left at the third light onto Madison Rd. At the first traffic light turn left into the Shopping Center. The Library, a large, brick, one-story, building is just ahead on the left. Turn into first parking on the left and right again.
> **(540) 825.8691   Culpepperhistory.info/resources**

ORIGINAL DOCUMENTS

Culpeper County Clerk of the Circuit Court has most of the original documents dating from its founding in 1749. The Clerk's Office and Record Room are in the Courthouse building. The Clerk maintains birth records 1864-1896, and 1912-1917; death records 1864-1896;

marriage records from 1781; land and probate records from 1749; and court records from 1831.

FIND IT: 135 West Cameron Street, Culpeper, VA 22710
From the Library turn right back onto Madison Road and continue straight into Main Street about 1 mile and turn left onto Cameron Street. The Annex building that houses the Record Room is at the end of the block on the corner. Park in the lot diagonal to the building. Enter through security, go up to the second floor. The Record Room is just down the hall.
(540) 727.3438

GOOD TO KNOW

The "Graffiti House" 19484 Brandy Road, Brandy Station, VA 22714 was built in 1858 in the village of Brandy Station and is one of few modest pre-Civil War dwellings to survive intact to this day. Because of its location the house was used extensively by both Union and Confederate armies. After the great cavalry battle at Brandy Station on June 9, 1863, the house served as a Confederate hospital. Later, Federal troops occupied the building when the Army of the Potomac camped in Culpeper during the winter of 1863-64. The plaster walls on the second floor of the house are covered with an outstanding and unique collection of charcoal graffiti left by soldiers from both armies. In addition to the graffiti, the house includes a small museum and serves as a visitor center for the Brandy Station battlefield. **(540) 727.7718 brandystationfoundation.com**

Museum of Culpeper History, 113 South Commerce Street, Culpeper, VA 22710 In the Old Train Depot the visitor will find exhibits about Historic Culpeper as well as a gift shop.
(540) 829.1749 culpepermuseum.com

CUMBERLAND COUNTY

Cumberland County was formed in 1749 from Goochland County. The county is named for William Augustus, Duke of Cumberland, and second son of King George II of Great Britain. The county seat is Cumberland.

 ## WHERE TO START

FAMILY RESEARCH

The Cumberland County Historical Society does not have a home base and the local library does not have genealogical files. The researcher would do well to visit the Historical Society in the parent county of Goochland.

> **FIND IT: 2875 River Road West, Goochland, VA 23103**
> (see Goochland County for directions)
> **(804) 556.3966   goochlandhistory.org**

ORIGINAL DOCUMENTS

Cumberland County Clerk of the Circuit Court has most of the original documents dating from its founding in 1749. The Clerk's Office and Record Room are in the Courthouse building. They have the following records: wills, deeds, marriages and court order books.

> **FIND IT: 1 Courthouse Circle, PO Box 8, Cumberland, VA 23040.** From Richmond make your way to VA-288 South and follow it to US-60 W. Turn right and stay on this road through the county of Powhatan. You will pass the Powhatan Courthouse which was once a part of Cumberland. Continue on US-60W until you reach Cumberland. The Courthouse faces Route 60. The Circuit Court Clerk's Office and Record Room can be entered directly through a door to the right of the main Courthouse entrance.
> **(804) 492.4442**

GOOD TO KNOW

Bear Creek Lake State Park is located 4.5 miles northwest of the town of Cumberland. Bear Creek Lake features overnight cabins, a lodge, permanent camp sites, and picnic shelters. Swimming and boating are allowed at the lake, and boat rentals are available. The park also has trails for hiking and running. **dcr.virginia.gov.state-parks/bear-creek-lake**

The 16,233-acre Cumberland State Forest is north of U.S. Route 60, west of State Route 45 and bordered on the west by the Willis River. There are two self-guided trails at Cumberland State Forest that are open for walking, hiking, horses, and mountain bikes. These are the **Cumberland Multi-Use Trail (14 miles)** and the **Willis River Hiking Trail (16-miles).** The State forest also features five lakes which may be fished from with a Virginia State fishing license, including: **Oak Hill Lake, Bear Creek Lake, Winston Lake, Arrowhead Lake, and Bonbrook Lake.**

DICKENSON COUNTY

Dickenson County was formed in 1880 from parts of Wise, Russell, and Buchanan Counties. Dickenson County is the youngest county in the Commonwealth. It was named for William Dickenson, a delegate to the Virginia Assembly. Its nickname is the "Baby County". The county seat is Clintwood.

 **WHERE TO START**

FAMILY RESEARCH

Dickenson County Historical Society:
The Society is the best place to start for family research. They have their own building and resource room. The Historical Society has available to the public local genealogy books, local history books, archived material of E. J. and Hetty Sutherland, and Bill Anderson, photos and displays. There are various other records and materials available for research.

> **FIND IT: 128 FFA Street, Clintwood, VA 24228**
> From I-81 S take exit 17 and turn right onto US-58ALT. In about 1 mile turn left onto US-11. Take the 3rd right onto Russell Road NW. In another mile bear right onto US-19N. Go about 12 miles and turn left onto US-58ALTW (again). Go 27 miles and exit #1 onto Front Street W. Take the 3rd left onto Laurel Ave/VA-72. In 10 miles merge with Coeburn Road to the right. In about ½ mile take the first left to stay on Coeburn Rd/ VA-72. In about 7 miles turn right onto Dickenson Hwy. In 1 ½ miles turn right onto Ralph Cummings Ave and take the 1st left onto FFA Street. The Society is the 1st building on the right.
> **(276) 926.6355   dchsva.org**

The Jonnie B. Deel Memorial Library also has a history section of books many of which were once a part of the Historical Society's collection.

FIND IT: 198 Chase Street, Clintwood, VA, 24228
From the Historical Society go back to Dickenson Hwy and
turn right. Follow it around to Chase Street. Turn left. Library
is ahead on the right. **(276) 926.6617**

ORIGINAL DOCUMENTS

Dickenson County Clerk of the Circuit Court has most of the
original documents dating from its founding in 1880. The Record Room
is on the first floor of a beautiful, red brick, white columned Courthouse
building. Ask about copies and cameras.

>**FIND IT: 194 Main Street, Clintwood, VA, 24228**. From
>the Historical Society go back to Dickenson Hwy and turn right.
>Take the 3rd left onto Clintwood Main Street. The Courthouse
>is ahead on the right. **(276) 926.1676**

GOOD TO KNOW

Dickenson County is home to world-famous bluegrass music
legend **Ralph Stanley**, and Clintwood is home to the **Ralph Stanley
Museum at 249 Main Street.**

The Phipps Memorial Garden is located on Chase Street across from
the library. There is also a small play area beside the parking lot of the
library.

Breaks Interstate Park: The Park's spectacular, deep river gorge is the
scenic centerpiece of Southwest Virginia and Eastern Kentucky. The park
grounds are open year round, with major facilities open from April 1 to
Dec. 21. Each season offers special delights for park visitors.
breakspark.com

The Chamber of Commerce is in the Doc Phipps house, Main Street,
Clintwood, VA 24228. **(276) 926.6074**

DINWIDDIE COUNTY

Dinwiddie County was formed in 1752 from Prince George County. The county is named for Robert Dinwiddie, Lieutenant Governor of Virginia. The county seat is Dinwiddie.

 **WHERE TO START**

FAMILY RESEARCH

Dinwiddie County Historical Society: The Dinwiddie County Historical Society currently occupies the historic Dinwiddie County Court House. They do have family files for the researcher.

> **FIND IT: 14103 Boydton Plank Road, Wilsons, VA 23849**
> From I-95 S take exit US-51 to merge onto I-85 S/ US-460. In about 15 miles take exit 53 toward Dinwiddie, keep right at the fork and merge onto VA-703. In about 1 mile turn left onto US-1 S/ Boydton Plank Road. In about ½ mile the Society is ahead on the left. Call ahead for an appointment.
> **(804) 469.5346**

ORIGINAL DOCUMENTS

Dinwiddie County Clerk of the Circuit Court has few records prior to 1833. **They were destroyed in 1865. One plat book, one order book, and one judgment book survive. B**irth and death records exist from 1865-1896, while marriage, wills and deeds exist from 1833.

> **FIND IT: 14008 Boydton Plank Road, Dinwiddie, VA 23841**
> From the library go back west on US-1. Cross Main Street and watch for the new Administration Building on the left. Enter through security. The Clerk's Office and Record Room are on the second floor. There is plenty of parking in front. **(804) 469.4540**

GOOD TO KNOW

The Appomattox Regional Library in Hopewell, VA (Prince George County) has a genealogy room with family files and other resources about Dinwiddie County. A good place to begin if the Dinwiddie Historical Society isn't open. See Prince George County for directions to this Library.

Pamplin Historical Park and The National Museum of the Civil War Soldier! Listed on the National Register of Historic Places, a Virginia Historic Landmark, and a National Historic Landmark, Pamplin Historical Park is recognized as one of America's premier historical attractions and as the most innovative Civil War history park in the country. **pamplinpark.org**

Poplar Grove National Cemetery: "Where Valor Proudly Sleeps". **8005 Vaughan Road, Dinwiddie, VA 23841** Places like Poplar Grove National Cemetery reflect the tragedy of the American Civil War. It is closed for burials but the grounds are open every day.

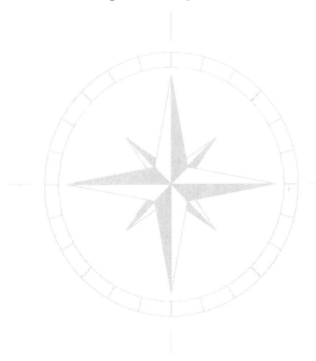

ESSEX COUNTY

Essex County was formed in 1692 from the old Rappahannock County, Virginia (not to be confused with the present day Rappahannock County, Virginia). The county is named for the English shire, or perhaps for the Earl of Essex. The county seat is Tappahannock.

## WHERE TO START

FAMILY RESEARCH

Essex County is fortunate to have 3 sites for genealogy research. **The Essex County Public Library** is the best place to begin.

> **FIND IT: Essex County Public Library, 117 North Church Lane, Tappahannock, VA 22560** From I-64 E exit #192 onto US-360 E. Follow this road for about 44 miles into Tappahannock. Continue on to the Library on Church Lane/ US-360 just past the Marsh Street intersection on the right. Park in front. **(804) 443.4945**

The Essex County Museum and Historical Society has an archival library worth visiting but reservations are necessary to access the records. They are very accommodating.

> **FIND IT: Essex County Museum and Historical Society, 218 Water Lane, Tappahannock, VA 22560.** From the library turn back left onto Church Street, then left onto Prince Street. Cross Water Lane and park on the left. The Museum entrance is just down Water Lane on the right, a pretty brick building with green awnings. [**research@echms.org** for reservations] **(804) 443.4690 ecmhs.org**

ORIGINAL DOCUMENTS

Essex County Clerk of the Circuit Court has most records from 1692 to date. This office is the repository for seventeenth-century records of old Rappahannock County, Virginia.

> **FIND IT: 305 Prince Street, Tappahannock, VA 22560**
> From the Museum go back along Prince Street and turn right onto Cross Street for parking. The entrance to the Clerk's office faces Cross Street. **(804) 443.3541**

GOOD TO KNOW

Captain John Smith landed here in 1608, but was driven back to his ship by the local Indians. Tappahannock is an Indian name meaning "on the rise and fall of water." Rappahannock, the name of the river, means "rise and fall of water." In the early 1600's Jacob Hobbs established a waterhouse and trading post here. Today, thirteen sites are included in Tappahannock's Historic Landmark District.
essex-virginia.org

Scots Arms Tavern – 1680
Ritchie House - 1706
Henley House (Emerson's Ordinary) - 1718
Beale Memorial Baptist Church - 1728
Anderton House - 1760
McCall-Brockenbrough House - 1763
The Old Debtor's Prison - 1769
Customs House - 1800
The Old Clerk's Office - 1808
Essex County Courthouse - 1848
St. John's Episcopal Church - 1849
St. Margaret's Hall - 1850
Roane-Wright-Trible House – 1850

FAIRFAX COUNTY

Fairfax County was formed in 1742 from the northern part of Prince William County. It was named for Thomas Fairfax, 6th Lord Fairfax of Cameron, proprietor of the Northern Neck. The county seat is Fairfax.

 **WHERE TO START**

FAMILY RESEARCH

Fairfax County is a treasure trove of resources for the genealogist.
The Virginia Room of the City of Fairfax Regional Library: An excellent place to begin. Special hours have been set up on the 2nd and 4th weeks of the month to help with Fairfax County Research.

> **FIND IT: Virginia Room, Fairfax City Regional Library, 10360 North Street, Fairfax, VA 22030-2514** From I-95 N exit #160B onto VA-123N toward Occoquan/Lake Ridge. Follow VA-123 for about 14 miles. Turn right onto North St. The Library is ahead on the left. Open 7 days a week.
> **(703) 293.6227x6   fairfaxcounty.gov/library**

ORIGINAL DOCUMENTS

Fairfax County Clerk of the Circuit Court has most all of the County records.

> **FIND IT: 4110 Chain Bridge Road, Fairfax, VA 22030**
> From the Library on the corner of Old Lee Highway and North Street make your way back onto VA-123 the way you came. About 4 blocks down, turn right onto Judicial Drive. Follow Judicial Drive to the stop sign, turn right on Page Avenue which leads to the public parking garage. When you leave the garage, walk up Page Ave to the main entrance to the Courthouse. Enter through security. The Record Room is located on the 3rd floor.
> **(703) 691.7320**

GOOD TO KNOW

City of Alexandria Library Special Collections, 717 Queen Street Alexandria, Virginia 22314-2420. Special Collections has many resources to help the genealogist research his or her family's history. The collection focuses mainly on material relating to Alexandria and Virginia in general, but other genealogy resources are available as well.
(703) 746.1720   alexandria.lib.va.us

The Fairfax Genealogical Society provides education and training for family history researchers in the Fairfax County area. **Fairfax Genealogical Society, Inc. PO Box 2290, Merrifield, VA 22113. fxgs.org**

There are countless numbers of things to do and see historically and outdoorsy in and around Fairfax. Two of the most popular are listed here.

Mount Vernon, 3200 Mount Vernon Memorial Highway, Mount Vernon, VA 22309 home of George Washington, the first president of the United States. **(703) 780.2000   mountvernon.org**

National Air and Space Museum Steven F. Udvar-Hazy Center 14390 Air and Space Museum Parkway, Chantilly, VA 20151 A companion to the Museum on the Mall in D.C., this museum houses the Space Shuttle Discovery and thousands of other aviation and space artifacts in two huge hangars.
(703) 572.4118   airandspace.si.edu/visit/udvar-hazy-center

FAUQUIER COUNTY

Fauquier County was formed in 1759, from Prince William County. It is named for Francis Fauquier, Lieutenant Governor of Virginia. The county seat is Warrenton.

 **WHERE TO START**

FAMILY RESEARCH
The Virginiana Room of the Fauquier County Public Library is the best place to begin.

> **FIND IT: 11 Winchester Street, Warrenton, VA 20186** From I-95 N, exit #133 onto US 17 toward Warrenton. In about 27 miles bear slight right onto US-15/ James Madison Hwy. In about 5 miles turn left to stay on Madison Hwy/US-15 Bus. Go about 2 more miles through Warrenton. Turn right onto Culpepper Street which ends at Main Street. Turn left onto Main, then right onto Alexandria Pike. Library parking is straight ahead down the hill on the left. From this lot you may enter the library's back door. Go to the 1st floor and ask for assistance at the reference desk. There is limited street parking anywhere in this part of town. Watch for time limits even in the public lots.
> **(540) 422.8500   library.faquier county.gov**

ORIGINAL DOCUMENTS

Fauquier County Clerk of the Circuit Court has prepared an excellent guide to records and their holdings in the record room. Most all of the records exist from 1759.

FIND IT: 29 Ashby Street, Warrenton, VA 20186 From the Library parking lot on Alexandria Pike, come back toward the Courthouse and bear right onto Main/ Waterloo Street. Take the first left onto Ashby Street. Turn left onto Lee St. for parking. The Clerk's Office entrance faces Ashby St. **(540) 422.8110**

GOOD TO KNOW

Go to *visitfauquier.com* to download a map of the historic sites in Warrenton. The visitor can tour by foot or by car.

Afro-American Historical Association, 4243 Loudoun Avenue, The Plains, Virginia 20198 In addition to the research facility which holds thousands of files for genealogical research, this community museum's exhibits hold valuable photographs and artifacts, important to Fauquier County's local history, as well as our Nation's history. Check out the Virtual Museum online at the web address.
(540) 253.7488   aahafauquier.org

Fauquier Heritage Society; John Gott Library, 4110 Old Winchester Rd, Marshall, VA 20116 The Fauquier Heritage Society for Local History and Genealogy, Inc. created an archival library to house genealogical and historical materials on the history of Fauquier County. The John K. Gott Library offers 3,500 volumes of research resources.
(540) 364.3440   fhpf.org

Weston Farmstead, 4447 Weston Road, Casanova, Virginia 20139 Weston, an early-American treasure, is one of Fauquier County's most completely preserved nineteenth-century farmsteads. The property goes back to Robert "King" Carter's land grant, while the present-day farmhouse, originally a 2-story log cabin, was built by the Fitzhugh family sometime around 1817. Weston retains its rare collection of ten original agricultural and domestic outbuildings: log kitchen, smokehouse, overseer's cabin; dairy, corn crib, blacksmith shop, tool shed/workroom, two barns and a stable. **(540) 788.9220**

FLOYD COUNTY

Floyd County was formed from Montgomery County in 1831.
It was named for John Floyd, governor of Virginia at that time.
In 1870 a portion of Franklin County was added to Floyd County.
Its county seat is Floyd.

WHERE TO START

FAMILY RESEARCH

The Jessie Peterman Library is the best place to begin. Ask for the
Genealogy Room where you will find family files, Floyd County history
and much more to get you started.

> **FIND IT: 321 West Main Street, Floyd, VA** From I-81 S, take
> the US-8 Floyd/Christiansburg exit and keep left on the ramp
> toward Floyd/Riner. Follow US-8 for about 20 miles. Turn right
> onto West Main St. The Library is ahead on the left.
> **(540) 745.2947**

ORIGINAL DOCUMENTS

Floyd County Clerk of the Circuit Court has all of the records
from 1831 available for research. The Historical Society has put all the
marriages into a searchable database available in the Clerk's Office.

> **FIND IT: 100 East Main Street, Room 200, Floyd, VA 24091**
> From the Library turn right back on to West Main Street. Cross
> N. Locust Street/ US-8. The Courthouse is on the corner and
> parking is on the street. Enter through the front. The Clerk's
> Office is around to the right. Ask for the Record Room.
> **(540) 745.9330**

GOOD TO KNOW

Floyd County has a strong music and literary tradition. Best known is the Friday Night Jamboree held at The Floyd Country Store. Floyd County is featured on the Virginia Heritage Music Trail called "The Crooked Road." Floyd is the home of an annual music festival called FloydFest.

Floyd County Historical Society Museum 217 North Locust Street Floyd, VA 24091 has created a self-guided historic walking tour of the Town of Floyd. Brochures are available at the Chamber of Commerce, Floyd Country Store, and The Jacksonville Center for the Arts. **(540)745.3247 floydhistoricalsociety.org**

Blue Ridge Parkway Floyd County has the longest stretch of Parkway in Virginia. **Blue Ridge Parkway.org**

Mabry Mill is an Historic Grist Mill. Self-guided tours/exhibits on rural Appalachian life. At Mile Post 176 on the Blue Ridge Parkway.

Buffalo Mountain Natural Area Preserve is widely recognized as one of Virginia's greatest natural heritage treasures. Go to **dcr.virginia.gov** and search for Buffalo Mountain.

Rock Churches in Floyd: Constructed from native stones from the Blue Ridge Mountains, the beautiful rock churches in Floyd are three of the six rock churches built in the first half of the 20th century under the leadership of Rev. Bob Childress. **rockchurches2.chillsnet.org/index**

FLUVANNA COUNTY

Fluvanna County was formed from Albemarle County in 1777. The County was named for the Fluvanna River, the name given to the James River west of Columbia. Fluvanna means "Anne's River" in honor of Queen Anne of England. The county seat is Palmyra.

WHERE TO START

FAMILY RESEARCH
The Archives are located at Maggie's House in the village of Palmyra. Appointments can be made with Tricia Johnson for research Tuesdays and Wednesdays from 1-4 pm.

> **FIND IT: 14 Stone Jail Street, Palmyra VA 22963** From Richmond follow I-64 W about 50 miles. Exit #136 and turn left onto US-15/James Madison Hwy toward Palmyra. In about 9 miles turn right onto Court Square/ Rte. 1004. This will take you past the Stone Jail and Maggie's House on the left. To park, drive to the intersection with Main Street. Turn left and park on the right. Walk back and up across the road to Maggie's House for research and The Stone Jail.
> **(434) 589.7910   fluvannahistory.org**

ORIGINAL DOCUMENTS

Fluvanna County Clerk of Circuit Court has all of the records from 1777 available for research, including family cemeteries and burial records.

> **FIND IT: 72 Main Street, Palmyra, Virginia 22963** From Maggie's House follow the sidewalk down to the lower level. As you face the Courthouse the Record Room is on the right.
> **(434) 591.1971**

GOOD TO KNOW

On the **walking tour of Court Square** in the historic village, the 1830 Courthouse sits overlooking the Confederate Park and faces the new Courthouse. Visit **fluvannahistory.org /walking tour** to download a brochure.

Scottsville, VA is an historic James River town between Fluvanna and Albemarle Counties. Also known as the "Scottsville Historic District," it has 153 buildings of nationally recognized historic significance. The town was originally called Scott's Landing and built on an area known as Horseshoe Bend. Later Scottsville became a center of Civil War activity. **Hatton Ferry** is a poled cable ferry located 5.5 miles west of Scottsville, Virginia on the James River. It is the last poled ferry in the United States. The ferry crosses the river upstream of Scottsville between Albemarle County and Buckingham County. The Ferry operates on a weekend schedule from April to October.

The Piedmont Crossroads Visitor Center for Louisa, Fluvanna, & Orange Counties is located in the Best Western Inn and Suites at Zion's Crossroads, VA 22942.

Further genealogy resources for Fluvanna can be found at the Albemarle County Historical Society and the Goochland County Historical Society. See each county page for directions.

FRANKLIN COUNTY

The county was formed in 1785 from parts of Bedford and Henry counties. It was named for Benjamin Franklin. The county seat is Rocky Mount.

 WHERE TO START

FAMILY RESEARCH

Franklin County Public Library in Rocky Mount, contains a local history section known as the "The Mann Room." The materials in this room cover Franklin County as well as Bedford and Henry counties. You will find court records, histories, military, schools and family records. There is an on-staff genealogist to help.

> **FIND IT: 355 Franklin Street Rocky Mount, Virginia 24151**
> From Richmond make your way southwest out of town toward Amelia and Farmville, VA on US-460 W. Follow US-460 and exit with a left turn onto VA-122 toward Bedford, VA. In about 34 miles turn right onto Old Franklin Turnpike. In about 1 mile the Turnpike becomes Tanyard Road. In about ½ mile turn right onto Pell Ave. In another ½ mile or so turn right onto N Main Street. Take the first left onto Franklin Street. The Library is ahead on the left. Park on the street.
> **(540) 483-3098x0   franklincountyfriends.org**

ORIGINAL DOCUMENTS

Franklin County Clerk of the Circuit Court has original records from 1785.

FIND IT: 275 S. Main Street, Suite 212 Rocky Mount, VA 24151 From the Library continue on down Franklin Street and take the first right onto College Street and then the first left back onto Franklin Street/ Warren Street. Take the first left onto West Court Street and the second right onto South Main Street. The Courthouse is ahead on the left. Park behind the building. Enter through the front and turn right. The Clerk's Office is down the hall on the left. Ask for the Record Room. This record room is carpeted and very well kept. **(540) 483.3065**

GOOD TO KNOW

In the 20th century during Prohibition, the locals named Franklin County the "Moonshine Capital of the World", because moonshine production and bootlegging were important forms of income. As of 2000, the local chamber of commerce formally adopted the title since Moonshine is still being made in the area.

Blue Ridge Institute & Farm Museum is the official State Center for Blue Ridge Folklore. It highlights the folk traditions of western Virginia, old and new including the Legendary Bootleg Liquor of Virginia's Blue Ridge Mountains. It is the eastern gateway of the Crooked Road Music Trail at 20 Museum Dr., Ferrum, VA 24088 **(540) 365.4416   blueridgeinstitute.org**

Smith Mountain Lake can be reached in the north east corner of Franklin County. **smith-mountain-lake.com**

FREDERICK COUNTY

The county was formed in 1743 by the splitting of Orange County. It was named for Frederick Louis, Prince of Wales, and the eldest son of King George II. It is Virginia's northernmost county. The county seat is Winchester.

 **WHERE TO START**

FAMILY RESEARCH

The Stewart Bell Jr. Archives Room of the Handley Regional Library has an extensive collection of local histories, genealogy files, and books about specific families. A Surname index lists individual family names from more than 400 family trees in the collection. Plan to stay awhile. Note that the hours for the archives are a bit different from the Library hours.

> **FIND IT: 100 West Piccadilly St, Winchester, VA 22601**
> The Library sits on the corner of Piccadilly and Braddock Streets. From Richmond most maps suggest I-95 to US-17 toward Warrenton. Continue to follow US-17/ US-15. It will eventually become James Madison Highway/US-17 N. Merge onto I-66/ US-17 N. In about 5 miles exit 23 onto US-17 N/Winchester Road toward Delaplane. In about 8 miles turn left onto US-17 N/John Mosby Hwy. In about 18 miles turn right onto S Cameron Street. In less than a mile turn left onto East Piccadilly Street. The library is ahead on the right. Street parking is usually available along Piccadilly Street.
> **(540) 662.9041 x17   handleyregional.org**

ORIGINAL DOCUMENTS

Frederick County Clerk of the Circuit Court has all of the records from 1743 available for research. Check in with a deputy clerk and ask for the record room.

FIND IT: 5 North Kent Street, Winchester, VA 22601 From the Library go back east on Piccadilly Street. Cross Braddock and Cameron Streets. Turn right onto North Kent Street. This is a large brick Judicial Center, not a traditional courthouse. The Winchester Star building is across the street. There is parking on both sides of the street. Enter through security. The Clerk's Offices for the City of Winchester and for Frederick County are on the first floor.

GOOD TO KNOW

All of the following places can be found in and around Winchester. For more information go to <u>visitwinchesterva.com</u>

Civil War History
Civil War Orientation Center
Old Court House Museum
Stonewall Jackson's HQtrs
Winchester National Cemetery

Historic Manor Homes
Belle Grove Plantation
Glen Burnie Historic House
Long Branch Plantation

Museums
Abram's Delight Museum
Feltner Museum at 9 Ct Square
George Washington's Office
Godfrey Miller Historic Home
Shenandoah Valley Museum
Newtown History Center
Patsy Cline Historic House
Shenandoah Valley Children's Discovery Museum
Loudoun Street Pedestrian Mall
Mount Hebron Cemetery
Korean War Memorial   POW-MIA Memorial

GILES COUNTY

Giles County was formed in 1806 from Montgomery, Monroe, Wythe, and Tazewell counties. The county is named for William Branch Giles, governor of Virginia, who was born in Amelia County in 1762. The county seat is Pearisburg.

 ## WHERE TO START

FAMILY RESEARCH

The Research Office at the Giles County Historical Society contains a treasure-trove of information regarding the history of Giles County. Research materials include genealogy and history books, files of family information, county records, maps, photographs, newspapers, and other information. Please contact them for an appointment as the office is only open one day per week, but they may be able to accommodate you.

> **FIND IT: 208 North Main Street, Pearisburg, VA 24134** From I-81 take the US-460 Christiansburg/Blacksburg exit 118C-B-A and merge onto US-460 W towards Blacksburg. Follow US-460 W for about 33 miles then take the US-460 BUS E/VA-100 S/ Pearisburg exit. Loop around onto Route 460 Access Road which becomes N Main St. The Society Complex is ahead on the left. Look for the sign out front and turn in the driveway.
> **(540) 921.1050   gilescountyhistorical.org**

ORIGINAL DOCUMENTS

Giles County Clerk of the Circuit Court has all the original records available for research. The General Index to wills is not separated into Grantor/Grantee. All transfers are indexed in two volumes.

FIND IT: 501 Wenonah Ave., Pearisburg, VA 24134 The Giles County Court House is located just 2 blocks from The Giles County Historical Society Museum Complex. Continue down Main Street and take the 2nd left onto Wenonah Ave. The Courthouse is on the left.

GOOD TO KNOW

Giles County is the location of **Mountain Lake**, one of only two natural fresh water lakes in Virginia. The Lake drains into Little Stony Creek, which passes over "The Cascades", a spectacular waterfall, before reaching the New River. Contact the Mountain Lake Conservancy.
(540) 626.7121   mtnlakeconservancy.org

Cascade Falls About 150,000 visitors a year visit the Cascades. Without question, Cascade Falls is one of the most beautiful waterfalls in Virginia and possibly on the entire East Coast. Jefferson National Forest, Pembroke, VA. **(540) 552.4641**

Three **beautiful covered bridges** are located in traditional country settings in Giles County:

Sinking Creek Bridge, a 70-foot-long red wooden bridge with a tin roof, built in 1916. Open to the public.

Not open to the public, but also in Giles: Link Farm Bridge, 50-ft. bridge, with red board sides and a sheet-metal roof, dating from 1912, and Reynold's Farm Bridge, 36-foot bridge built in 1919. It can be viewed from US 42.

GLOUCESTER COUNTY

Gloucester County was formed from York County in 1651.
It was named for Henry Stuart, Duke of Gloucester (third son of
King Charles I of England). The county seat is Gloucester.

 WHERE TO START

FAMILY RESEARCH

Gloucester County Public Library is the best place to begin. The
Gloucester Genealogical Society maintains a wealth of resources here
such as Gloucester census, death records, marriages, cemeteries, tax
records and more.

> **FIND IT: 6920 Main Street, Gloucester, VA 23061.** From
> I-64 exit # 220 onto VA-33 E toward West Point. Follow VA-33
> E for about 14 miles then turn right onto VA-14E. Follow VA-
> 14E for about 6 miles then turn right onto George Washington
> Memorial Hwy/US-17 S/VA-14. In about 1 mile keep left onto
> Main Street. In about 1 more mile turn right to stay on Main
> Street. The Library is about 1 mile ahead on the right in the
> Main Street Shopping Center. It is the first building on the left
> end of the mall.
> **(804) 693.2998   glouchesterva.info/library**

ORIGINAL DOCUMENTS

Gloucester County Clerk of the Circuit Court has records
from 1865 to the present. It suffered heavy record loss in 1820 and
then again in 1865. Note that Deeds and Wills are indexed into Grantor
Books but actual wills are bound into Will Books.

FIND IT: 7400 Justice Drive, Gloucester, VA 23061 From the Library turn left back on to onto Main Street. Follow Main Street through a round-about and turn right onto Justice Drive. The Courthouse is ahead on the right. Enter through the front and go the 3rd floor for the Record Room. **(804) 693.2502**

GOOD TO KNOW

The Gloucester Museum of History, 6539 Main Street, Gloucester, Virginia 23061 is located in the Historic Botetourt Building. **(804) 693.1234**

Thomas Jefferson wrote early works for Virginia and colonial independence at **Rosewell Plantation**, home of John Page (his close friend and fellow student at the College of William and Mary). Gloucester County is nicknamed the "Daffodil Capital of the World"; it hosts an annual daffodil festival, parade and flower show.

African American Heritage Trails - a driving tour of selected African American historic sites in Gloucester County. Visit 8 sites that have significantly influenced Gloucester's development and culture and the overall African American culture. **gloucesterva.info** choose Visitors and then self-guided tours.

Historic Court Circle: Within the brick walls of the Green is one of the oldest Courthouses still in use in Virginia; a Debtors Prison, Jail and two Clerks of the Court offices.

Virginia Birding and Wildlife Trail
gloucesterva.info/tourism

GOOCHLAND COUNTY

Goochland County is fortunate to have most all of its court documents since it was created in 1728 from Henrico County. As many as 8 counties and two states would eventually be formed from Goochland County. Thomas Jefferson was actually born in Goochland County in 1743, a year before Albemarle County was established from Goochland. His father, Peter, and his mother, Jane Randolph, were also from Goochland County and were married here. The county seat is Goochland.

 WHERE TO START

FAMILY RESEARCH

The Goochland County Historical Society: This is the best place to begin for all researchers. The library contains an extensive family file collection and volunteers who are most helpful to the novice researcher. All of the family files are indexed in a searchable data base. There is a Wi-Fi connection and the copy fee is 25 cents. All of the chancery records are now on line and can be accessed from a computer at the Center. Any transcriptions that have been published will be found here as well.

> **FIND IT: 2875 River Road West, Goochland, VA 23063**
> From Richmond all roads west can lead to Goochland!
> From I-64 exit 159 (Gum Spring) to follow US-522 toward Goochland. At the traffic light turn right. Watch for signs for a left turn to stay on US-522. In about 6 miles the road will dead-end. Turn left. At the traffic light, turn left again onto VA-6 east. Go through the Court House Village of Goochland. The Society Center is in a brick house on the south side of VA-6 (River Road West) under the water tower.
> **(804) 556.3966   goochlandhistory.org**

ORIGINAL DOCUMENTS

Goochland County Clerk of the Circuit Court has complete records from 1728. Here the original wills are in the Deed Books. There are no separate Will Books for Goochland. An alphabetical index for deeds and wills is bound into the Grantor books and are on shelves for easy access. In some cases the alphabetical listing is continued in the far back of the index book. All the extant Marriage Bonds have been copied, indexed, and put into spiral binders. Order Books 1 – 6 have been transcribed.

> **FIND IT: 2938 River Road West, Goochland, VA 23063**
> The Record Room is on the bottom floor of Building B which sits on the north side of US 6 just east of the Courthouse. From the Historical Society turn left on to Rte. 6 and travel about .25 miles. Turn right at the brick wall that surrounds the Courthouse. **(804) 556.5353**

GOOD TO KNOW

The Goochland Courthouse Complex: Designed by Dabney Cosby, architect for Thomas Jefferson, the courthouse is essentially the same as when it was built in 1823. The 1820s stone jail is being restored; a welcome center will be located in the Old Clerk's Office and a walkway with interpretative signage will surround the Green.

Tuckahoe Plantation: 12601 River Road, Richmond, VA 23238   The boyhood home of Thomas Jefferson is a National Historic Landmark. House tours are by appointment.
(804) 971.8329   tuckahoeplantation.com

Maidens Bridge over the James is just east of the Historical Society on US Route 6. It was very near this location that a ferry brought people across the river when the County was established in 1728. This was also the last stop for the Kanawah Canal for several years. Just across the railroad bridge along the James River and on the west side of Maidens Road is **Tucker Park at Maidens Crossing.** There is a hiking trail with interpretative signage along the river.

GRAYSON COUNTY

Grayson County was founded in 1793 from part of Wythe County. It was named for William Grayson, delegate to the Continental Congress from 1784 to 1787 and one of the first two U.S. Senators from Virginia. The county seat is Independence.

 **WHERE TO START**

FAMILY RESEARCH

Grayson County Public Library: has a special genealogy research area with extensive reference materials. Reference materials include book collections, censuses, and family files which have been donated to the library.

> **FIND IT: 147 S. Independence Ave, Independence, VA 24348**
> From I-81, take the US-11 S exit toward Wytheville. Merge onto E Main St. and follow for 2.7 miles. Turn left onto Grayson Rd/ US-21 S and go about 29 miles. Watch for the intersection of US-21 and US-58 at a traffic light. The Old Courthouse, home to the Office of Tourism, is on your left at this intersection. The library is straight ahead through the intersection on the left.
> **(276) 773.2761   wythegrayson.lib.va.us**

ORIGINAL DOCUMENTS

Grayson County Clerk of the Circuit Court has all of the records from1793 available for research. Check in with a clerk and ask for the record room.

> **FIND IT: 129 Davis Street, Independence, VA 24348** From the library go back into town to the intersection and turn right, just in front of the Old Courthouse. Take the next right. The

Courts Building will be on the left. Enter through the front. The Record Room is on the third floor. **(276) 773-2231**

GOOD TO KNOW

The Grayson County Heritage Foundation offers research support at the office on Thursdays and Fridays, April – October. 578 East Main Street in Independence, VA. (276) 773.2126. The web site offers an excellent guide to using the Record Room at the Courthouse. **graysonheritage.org**

Grayson County is home to the highest mountains in Virginia, Mt. Rogers at 5,729 feet and Whitetop Mountain at 5,520 feet. The summit of Whitetop can be reached by 4x4 vehicles. Park at a marked trailhead and hike the Appalachian Trail.

Woven Mountains and River Bends, Grayson County's Artisan Trail highlights the studios and shops of local artisans. The trail is designed to provide a unique cultural experience in the heart of Appalachia where world renowned craftsman produce pottery, fiddles, stained glass, portraits and other quality arts. **graysoncountyva.com**

The Crooked Road comprises 333 miles of a musical heritage trail unique to southwestern Virginia. The trail begins in Franklin County, Virginia on State Highway 58, and ends at Breaks Interstate Park on the Virginia/Kentucky border. Music jams are common in Grayson County on the longest stretch of The Crooked Road. **swva.org**

Hiking Trails include **Matthews State Forest; Iron Mountain; Fisher Peak Trail; New River Trail State Park; Lewis Fork Wilderness Trail; and the Virginia Creeper Trail** on top of Whitetop Mountain.

GREENE COUNTY

Greene County was formed in 1838 from Orange County. The county is named for American Revolutionary War hero Nathanael Greene. The county seat is Stanardsville.

WHERE TO START

FAMILY RESEARCH

Greene County Historical Society has numerous family histories, obituary files, as well as a large database of Greene County VA descendants.

> **FIND IT: 38 Court Street, P.O. Box 18, Stanardsville, Virginia 22973** Open Friday and Saturday or call for an appointment. They are very willing to help the researcher. **(434) 985.1409 greenehistory.org**

ORIGINAL DOCUMENTS

Greene County Clerk of the Circuit Court has all land and probate records from 1838.

> **FIND IT: 22 Court Square, Stanardsville, VA 22973** From I-64 W take the US-15 exit toward Gordonsville. Follow US-15 N/James Madison Hwy for about 19 miles. Turn right onto Celt Rd. Take the second right onto Stanard Rd. Take the first left onto Ford Ave. Take the first right onto Court St. 22 Court Street is on the right. The Clerk's Office is in the building to the right of the Courthouse on Court Square. **(434) 985.5208**

Since Greene County was once part of Orange County, the researcher is advised to consult the pages about Orange County and plan a visit there as well.

GOOD TO KNOW

In 1935, 14,619 acres of Greene County land was acquired by the State and given to the Federal Government for the formation of Shenandoah National Park, which is located in the Blue Ridge Mountains. It is estimated that a total of 285 county citizens were displaced by the dedication of the parkland.

A walking trail through the town of Stanardsville has been mapped with a brief history about each site. It is available from the Visitor Center in Ruckersville, VA or on line at **cometogreene.com**. Some of the sites in town are:

The Greene County Courthouse first built in1838
The Old County Jail
1858 Methodist Church
1840 Lafayette Hotel
1810 Evergreen Country House
The Bickers-Whitlock House
1815 house the oldest house still standing
A Queen Anne Victorian house built in 1892

GREENSVILLE COUNTY

Greensville County was formed in 1781 from Brunswick County. The county is probably named for Sir Richard Grenville, leader of the settlement on Roanoke Island, 1585. There is also belief that it may have been named after Nathanael Greene, a Major General of the Continental Army. The county seat is Emporia.

WHERE TO START

FAMILY RESEARCH

The Richardson Memorial Library: The Library is a part of the Meherrin Regional Library System. An on-line catalogue contains many of the family genealogy books that have been donated. The Library also maintains a vertical file of family folders which are available on request.

> **FIND IT: 100 Spring Street, Emporia, VA 23847.** From Richmond follow I-95 S about 56 miles. Exit 11A onto US-58 W/Atlantic Street. In about ½ mile turn right onto the US-58 By-Pass. In about ½ mile turn right onto N. Main Street. In another ½ mile turn right onto Spring Street. The Library is the brick building ahead on the left. There is plenty of parking. **(434) 634.2539   meherrinlib.org/directory**

ORIGINAL DOCUMENTS

Greensville County Clerk of the Circuit Court has land and will records from 1781.

> **FIND IT: 337 S. Main Street, Emporia, VA 23847** From the Library walk back one block to Main Street and turn left. The Courthouse is ahead on the left. Follow the sidewalk to the cannon which sits near the entrance to the Circuit Court Clerk's Office. There is ample street parking. **(434) 348.4215**

GOOD TO KNOW

Belfield-Emporia Historic District, also known as North Emporia, includes 41 buildings. Notable buildings include the **Hotel Virginia, the Bethlehem Building aka First National Bank of Emporia (1907), Petersburg and Danville Railroad passenger station, Pair's Furniture (c. 1904), and the H. T. Klugel Architectural Sheet Metal Work Building.**

Hicksford-Emporia Historic District, also known as Emporia, includes 36 buildings that date from the early 1900s. Notable buildings include the **Citizen's National Bank, the Widow's Son's Masonic Lodge, First Presbyterian Church, Emporia Elementary School, Emporia Armory, Greensville County Auditorium, and Emporia Post Office**. Built in 1929, **Greensville County Training School, 105 Ruffin Street**, also known as the Greensville County Learning Center, is a historic Rosenwald school building.

The Old Merchants and Farmers Bank Building, 419 S. Main Street, facade features a galvanized sheet-metal cornice that may have been manufactured by H. T. Klugel. It is currently occupied by the Greensville-Emporia Historical Museum.

The County Courthouse, 337 S. Main Street, was built in 1831 by Daniel Lynch. The elaborate portico was added in the early 20th century. An 1894 clerk's office stands on the courthouse green. Some interior walls feature pressed-tin coverings made by the H. J. Klugel company.

Village View, 221 Briggs Street, also known as the Mansion House, was built about 1815, and substantially improved in 1826. It is a Federal style frame dwelling with a two-story front porch and exterior end chimneys. Village View served as a Confederate headquarters during the American Civil War and was used later by the owners of a boys' academy.

HALIFAX COUNTY

Halifax County was formed in 1752 from Lunenburg County. The county was named for George Montague-Dunk, 2nd Earl of Halifax. The county seat is Halifax.

 **WHERE TO START**

FAMILY RESEARCH

Halifax County – South Boston Public Library: The library features published works about local and regional history. It houses several important personal collections of papers and other documents including George Waldrep's catalogues of gravesites.

> **FIND IT: 177 S Main St., Halifax, VA 24558** From Richmond make your way to VA-288 south and exit US-360 towards Amelia, VA. In about 88 miles keep right onto VA-360 W. In about 7 miles VA-360 becomes Main Street. The Library is ahead on the left. Turn left at the dinosaur sculpture. The library is back off the road. There is lots of parking in front.
> **(434) 476.3357**

ORIGINAL DOCUMENTS

Halifax County Clerk of the Circuit Court has court documents including will books, deed books, and other official records that date back to 1752.

> **FIND IT: 8 S Main St. Halifax, VA 24558** The Courthouse faces Main Street and is about two blocks back along Main Street from the Halifax Library. Enter through the front of the building. The Clerk's Office is directly ahead.
> **(434) 476.6211**

GOOD TO KNOW

South Boston – Halifax County Museum of Fine Arts and History, 1540 Wilborn Avenue, South Boston, VA. The Research Center in the Museum is another place to research family genealogy. Resources available include newspaper archives, community histories, yearbooks, maps, pictures, and microfilms. The Museum is about 4 miles south of Halifax, VA. **(434) 572.9200**

discoverhalifaxva.com is the tourism website for Halifax County. A stop at the **Visitor's Center at 1178 Bill Tuck Highway** in South Boston is worth the time. Pick up a walking tour map while you are there. Some County highlights are:

The Prizery is an arts and cultural center located in a building where tobacco was "prized," or pressed layer by layer into hogshead barrels often weighing up to 1000 pounds.

The Virginia Piedmont Birding and Wildlife Trail maps focus on the natural and cultural heritage of county sites.

The Clarkton Bridge spans the 250 feet wide Staunton River connecting the counties of Halifax and Charlotte. The bridge stands 53' over the riverbed. It is a magnificent through-truss bridge. The entrance on the Halifax County side is on a winding road along a cliff.

The L. E. Coleman African American Museum is about two miles west of Halifax, VA. It is a non-profit arts facility dedicated to promoting artistic excellence that primarily reflects the culture of African-Americans of Halifax County.

HANOVER COUNTY

Hanover County was formed in 1720, from the area of New Kent County called St. Paul's Parish. It was so named because King George I of Great Britain was Elector of Hanover at the time. The county seat is Hanover Court House.

 ## WHERE TO START

FAMILY RESEARCH
Many records for Hanover County were burned during the American Civil War. The researcher would do well to include the Library of Virginia in any research efforts. There are common law papers and chancery papers after 1831.

Florence L Page Memorial Library has data about families of Hanover County including genealogies, old homes and cemeteries. This is a good place to start.

> **FIND IT: 17193 Mountain Road, Montpelier, VA 23192**
> From I-95 N exit onto I-295 N toward Charlottesville. In about 5 miles exit # 49 A and merge onto US-33 W (Mountain Road). The Library is about 14 miles ahead on the left just past the village of Montpelier in the historic Sycamore Tavern.
> **(804) 883.5355**

Hanover Branch Library has a Virginiana Section that contains family files and other reference materials.

> **FIND IT: 7527 Library Drive, Hanover, VA 23060** From I-95 take Exit 92 (Rt. 54 East) towards Hanover. Travel approximately 7 miles to the intersection with Rt. 301. Turn right onto Rt. 301. Travel approximately ½ mile and turn left onto Library Drive. The Library is ahead on the right.
> **(804) 365.6210 pamunkeylibrary.org/hanover**

ORIGINAL DOCUMENTS

Hanover County Clerk of the Circuit Court has complete records that date to 1865. Many court records, particularly deeds, wills, and marriage records, were destroyed by fire in Richmond on April 3, 1865.

> **FIND IT: 7507 Library Drive, Hanover, VA 23069** Follow the directions for the Branch Library. The Circuit Court Building is on the right at the corner of Library Drive and County Complex Road. The Clerk's Office is on the 2nd floor of the Circuit Court Building. **(804) 365.6120**

GOOD TO KNOW

Hanover County was the site of a number of **Civil War battles**, including the **Seven Days Battles of the Peninsula Campaign** and **Battle of Cold Harbor** in 1864.

The Barksdale Theatre was founded at the historic Hanover Tavern, becoming the nation's first dinner theatre and Central Virginia's first professional theatre. Barksdale continues to produce live theatre at the Tavern, as well as at several locations in Richmond. It is recognized today as Central Virginia's leading professional theatre. **va-rep.org**

Kings Dominion, Virginia's premier amusement park opened in 1975 in Doswell, VA.

Scotchtown is a plantation in Beaverdam, VA that was built by Charles Chiswell. Patrick Henry purchased Scotchtown in 1771 and lived there with his family until he was elected Governor of Virginia in 1776. **(804) 227.3500**

Cold Harbor Battlefield and National Cemetery, 6038 Cold Harbor Road, Mechanicsville, VA. 23111. **(804) 795.2031**

HENRICO COUNTY

Established as the Citie of Henricus in 1611 by the Virginia Company, Henrico became one of the eight original English shires (counties) in 1634. It was named for Prince Henry, eldest son of King James I and is one of the oldest counties in the United States. The county seat is Henrico.

 ## WHERE TO START

All county court records prior to 1655 and almost all prior to 1677 are missing. Many records were destroyed by British troops during the Revolutionary War. **Post–Revolutionary War** county court records exist. Almost all circuit superior court of law and chancery and circuit court records were destroyed by fire in 1865.

FAMILY RESEARCH

There is no repository of files specifically for Henrico County. The Library of Virginia is by far the best place to search. Goochland County was formed from Henrico in 1728. The Goochland Historical Society maintains a research library with family files and transcribed Henrico County wills and deeds.

> **FIND IT: The Library of Virginia, 800 East Broad Street, Richmond, VA 23219** Because Broad Street is one-way going west, the simplest way to reach The Library of Virginia is from I-64 East. Exit #74C, follow it up and around to Broad Street. Move into the right lane and turn right onto 9th Street. Move into the far left lane as the parking garage entrance is just ahead on the left. Turn left and left again to the ticket kiosk. An elevator will take you up to street level. Exit and then enter the library through the glass doors on the right. Be sure to get your ticket validated at the front desk before you leave.
> **(804) 692.3500   lva.virginia.gov**

ORIGINAL DOCUMENTS

Henrico County Clerk of the Circuit Court has county wills from 1781-1898 and Circuit Court wills from 1866 to the present.

> **FIND IT: 4301 E. Parham Road, Courthouse Bldg., Rm. 240, Henrico, VA 23228** From downtown Richmond, VA on I-64 W exit #185 onto US-33/Staples Mill Road. In about 2 ½ miles turn left onto E Parham Road. In about ½ mile turn left onto Prince Henry Drive. Take the next right and the next left into the parking lot. **(804) 501.4202**

GOOD TO KNOW

Henricus Citie Historical Park is an outdoor living-history museum where visitors interact with period-dressed historical interpreters of the English settlers and Virginia Indians. **(804)748.1613   henricus.org**

The Richmond National Battlefield Park contains the American Civil War battle sites of Chickahominy Bluffs, Malvern Hill Park and Fort Harrison. **(804) 771.2145   visithenrico.com**

Meadow Farm Museum is an 1860 historical farm that demonstrates 19th–century rural life. **(804) 501.2130**

Lewis Ginter Botanical Gardens was once a hunting ground for the Powhatan Tribe. View 50 acres of beautiful year-round gardens. **(804) 262.9887**

Wolf Creek Cherokee Museum, 7400 Osborne Turnpike, Henrico, VA 23231 is a newly opened museum with exhibits about life of the Cherokee in Southwest Virginia. **(804) 226.1002   wolfcreekcherokee.com**

HENRY COUNTY

The county was formed in 1777 from Pittsylvania County. The new county was initially named Patrick Henry County in honor of Patrick Henry, who was then serving as the first Governor of Virginia after independence. The county seat is Martinsville.

WHERE TO START

FAMILY RESEARCH

Bassett Historical Center: This is by far the best place to begin. The Center is an excellent resource for family history research in Henry, Patrick, Floyd, Franklin and Pittsylvania counties in Virginia, the city of Martinsville, Virginia, and Rockingham, Stokes and Surry counties in North Carolina. It is in the town of Bassett but not too far from the Courthouse in Martinsville.

> **FIND IT: 3964 Fairy Stone Park Hwy, Bassett, VA 24055**
> From Richmond find your way to VA-288S to US-360W toward Amelia County and then down to South Boston via US-360/15. Continue on to and around Danville towards Martinsville. This will merge with US-58. In about 20 miles, you can exit onto US-220 N around the city or remain on US-58Bus through Martinsville. US-58 will merge with VA-57. The Center is about 15 miles northwest of Martinsville on VA-57/Fairystone Park Highway. The website includes descriptions of collections.
> **(276) 629.9191   bassetthistoricalcenter.com**

ORIGINAL DOCUMENTS

Henry County Clerk of the Circuit Court has deeds and wills that date from 1777 in the record room. Marriages begin in 1778.

> **FIND IT: 3160 Kings Mountain Rd, Martinsville, VA 24112**
> From the Bassett Historical Center go back out to VA-57E turn left and take the first left onto VA-57/Main Street. Cross the river left onto VA-57/Main Street. Cross the river, stay on VA-57, which runs into Virginia Ave/ US-220. Turn left onto VA-174E/ Kings Mountain Road. In about 2 miles you will see on your left the Henry County Governmental Complex, which is beyond the Refuse Road/Jack Dalton Park intersection. Take the second left turn lane off of Kings Mountain Road into Courthouse parking. Enter through security. Please note no cameras, cellphones with cameras or scanning devices are allowed into the Courthouse.
> **(276) 634.4880**

GOOD TO KNOW

There are at least 8 museums in Martinsville and Henry County, including the **Museum of Natural History**, a **Communications Museum,** and the **Piedmont Art Museum**. Take a walk to explore the many works of public art found throughout the city. There are several uniquely painted Brontosaurus sculptures strategically located around town. Find out more at **visitmartinsville.com.**

HIGHLAND COUNTY

Highland County was formed in 1847 from Bath County and Pendleton County in what is now West Virginia. Highland was named for its lofty elevation. The county seat is Monterey.

 WHERE TO START

FAMILY RESEARCH

The Highland County Public Library is the best place in Monterey to begin any research after 1847. Prior to that time check records in neighboring Bath County, VA or Pendleton County, WV. This Library has a genealogy section with Family Histories, access to computer research and assistance with your search.

> **FIND IT: 31 N. Water Street, Monterey, VA 24465**. Follow I-64W to I-81S/Lexington. Take a left at the fork to merge onto I-81 S/I-64. In about 1 mile exit #220 to merge onto VA-262N around the city of Staunton. In about 7 miles exit onto US-250/ Churchville Ave and turn left. This road goes directly into the town of Monterey, VA. In about 41 miles turn right onto Water Street. The Library is ahead on the left.
> **(540) 468.2373 highlandlibrary.homestead.com**

The Highland County Historical Society is an excellent research facility but the open hours are less frequent than those of the Library. This library includes family histories, an extensive obituary file, folders on individual families, and a family tree and photo collection for the pioneer families that settled in the area prior to 1800. Research assistance is available.

> **FIND IT: 161 Mansion House Rd, McDowell, VA 24458**
> Follow directions toward Monterey. From the exit onto US-250, in about 30 miles, you'll cross the Bull Pasture River. Continue on to Hwy 654/ Doe Hill Road. Turn right and take the first left onto Mansion House Road. The Society is ahead on the right.
> **(540) 396-4478 highlandcountyhistory.com**

ORIGINAL DOCUMENTS

Highland County Clerk of the Circuit Court has all of the records available for research.

FIND IT: 165 W Main St Monterey, VA 24465.

The Record Room is in the Courthouse. Follow the directions to the Public Library. From there go back to Main Street and turn left. The Courthouse is ahead through town on the left. Park on the street and enter through the front between the columns. The Clerk's Office is on the right. **(540) 468.2447**

GOOD TO KNOW

Highland County is often referred to as "Virginia's Switzerland". It is the least populous county in Virginia and has one of the highest average elevations east of the Mississippi River.

Take the Barn Quilt Tour while in Highland County. Beautiful quilt patterns have been painted onto barns across the county. Visit the Highland County Chamber of Commerce in Monterey for a map with directions to each barn. There is information about working farms that offer overnight and week-end accommodations as well.
(540) 468.2550   highlandcounty.org

Chamber of Commerce, 68 W Main Street, Montery, VA 24465

ISLE OF WIGHT COUNTY

Warrosquyoake Shire was renamed Isle of Wight County in 1637, after the island off the south coast of England. In 1732 a considerable portion of the northwestern part of the original shire was added to Brunswick County. In 1748 the entire county of Southampton was carved out of it. The county seat is Isle of Wight.

 WHERE TO START

FAMILY RESEARCH

The Blackwater Regional Library, Smithfield Branch: This library offers hundreds of valuable genealogy resources to researchers. Highlights include passenger lists, court records, marriage records, church and cemetery records, will and deed indexes, and war registers. They also have many books tracing local family lineage. This is the best place to begin.

> **FIND IT: 255 James Street, Smithfield, VA 23430** Follow I-95S to exit 47 and then turn left onto VA-629E/Rives Road. Go about 2 miles and turn right to stay on VA-629E and right again onto US-460. Go about 30 miles and turn left onto VA-620/Broadwater Road. In about 14 miles turn left onto US-258N/ Courthouse Hwy. This will become Main Street. In about 2 more miles turn left onto Cary Street, take the 1st right onto Grace Street, and then the 1st left onto James Street. The Library shares the building with the Paul D. Camp Community College. There are large signs for the Library.
> **(757) 357.2264   blackwaterlib.org/smithfield**

ORIGINAL DOCUMENTS

Isle of Wight County Clerk of the Circuit Court maintains a treasure called the Randall Booth Record Room. Many (most) of the records have been digitized and are available on-line as well as in the record room. There are records from the 1600's.

FIND IT: 17000 Josiah Parker Circle, Isle of Wight, VA 23397 From the Library return to James Street the way you came. Turn right, back onto Grace Street and follow it around to Main Street. Turn right and in about 6 miles **(watch carefully for this new road)** turn right onto Josiah Parker Circle. Follow it around to the 2-story Young Lane Courts Building. This is a new administration and courts complex. Enter through security at the front main entrance, take the elevator to the second floor, turn left and go to the end of the hall to the Clerk's Office. **(757)365.6233 co.isle-of-wight.us/clerk-of-the-circuit-court/genealogy**

GOOD TO KNOW

Smithfield & Isle of Wight Visitor Center, 319 Main Street, Smithfield, VA. The Visitor Center shares space with its tourism partner, the Arts Center @ 319. Be sure you stop in town at the Visitor Center for a historic walking tour map and for information on all the area attractions.
(757) 357.5182   visitsmithfieldisleofwight.com

St. Luke's Church, 14477 Benns Church Blvd., Smithfield, VA, built in 1632, is the nation's only original Gothic church and the oldest existing church of English foundation. It is a National Historic Landmark.   **(757) 357.3367**

JAMES CITY COUNTY

First settled by the English colonists in 1607 at Jamestown in the Virginia
Colony, the County was formally created in 1634 as James City Shire in
honor of King James I. James City County is one of five original shires
which exists within the same boundaries as originally formed. The county
seat is Williamsburg.

 ## WHERE TO START

FAMILY RESEARCH

Swem Library at the College of William and Mary At the
Swem Library, you'll find standard genealogy reference sources located
in the Virginia Genealogy Resource Center, plus hundreds of published
state and local sources, family papers, church records, and more. This is
an excellent library for research. Plan to stay awhile. Obtain a $5 cash
parking permit at the Parking Office when you arrive on campus.

> **FIND IT: 400 Landrum Drive, Williamsburg, VA 23185.**
> From Richmond follow I-64 E/ VA Beach about 43 miles. Exit
> #234 onto VA-199/Rte 646 toward Lightfoot and turn right onto
> VA-199. In about 8 miles turn left onto Rte 5/Jamestown Road.
> In about 1 mile turn left onto Ukrop Way. The Parking Office and
> Police Station is ahead on the left. There is a small parking lot to
> the right of the building. Purchase your $5 cash permit here.
> There is a parking deck here as well or continue along Campus
> Drive until it becomes Landrum Road. The Library is ahead
> on the right. There is parking along this street and a parking lot
> ahead on the left.
> **(757) 221.4636   www.swem.wm.edu/genealogy**

ORIGINAL DOCUMENTS

James City County Clerk of the Circuit Court has few court records prior to 1865. Some records from the 1850s are housed in the current Williamsburg-James City County Courthouse. Deed Book 1 and Will Book 1 both include some records from the 1850's.

> **FIND IT: Circuit Court, City of Williamsburg and County of James City, 5201 Monticello Ave., Suite 6, Williamsburg, VA 23188** From the Library on Landrum Drive, continue on a short distance and turn right onto Ukrop Way toward Wake Drive, about .4 mile. Turn left onto Compton Drive. In .6 mile turn left onto Monticello Ave. The Courthouse is ahead on the right. **(757) 564.2242**

GOOD TO KNOW

Williamsburg, and Jamestown are the two top spots in James City County. Yorktown is nearby.

Williamsburg:
visitwilliamsburg.com; colonialwillliamsburg.com

Jamestown: Historic Jamestowne Visitor Center, 1368 Colonial Pkwy,

Jamestown, VA 23081
historicjamestowne.org.

Jamestown and Yorktown:
historyisfun.org

KING AND QUEEN COUNTY

King and Queen County was formed in 1691 from New Kent County. The county is named for King William III and Queen Mary II of England. The county seat is King and Queen Court House.

 WHERE TO START

FAMILY RESEARCH

The Courthouse Tavern Museum has a small library on the second floor that is open when the Museum is open. Museum docents can often provide some assistance in your search for information. Books must be used in the library.

> **FIND IT: 146 Court House Landing Road, King and Queen Court House, Virginia 23085** Follow I-64 E and exit #192 to merge onto US-360 E. In about 20 miles turn right onto Rte 618. In about ½ mile turn right again to stay on Rte 618. In about 6 miles this road becomes Rte. 629. In about 2 more miles turn left onto VA-30 W and then right onto Rte. 629. In about 4 miles turn right onto Rte 634. In about 1 ½ miles this road will become Rte 633. In about 3 miles turn right onto Rte 632 which will become Rte 631. In about 3 miles bear right onto VA-14 E/ Trail Road. Turn right at the Fire Station and drive back to the Court Complex. The Museum is across the street from the Courthouse in a white frame building behind the Monument. **(804) 785.9558   kingandqueenmuseum.org**

ORIGINAL DOCUMENTS

King and Queen County Clerk of the Circuit Court has available deed books, marriage licenses and wills for the period 1864 to the present. There are also a few birth and death records available from the mid to late 1800's only, as well as transcribed census records.

> **FIND IT: 234 Allen's Circle, King and Queen Court House, VA 23085** The Clerk's office is next door to the museum. **(804) 785.5984**

GOOD TO KNOW

NEWTOWN was an Indian trail junction that became the "Great Cross Roads" of the colonial period. It was the site of taverns on the post road and the plantation of the Richards family became known as Newtown. There were several large schools in this vicinity in the post-revolutionary period. Near here was Spring Farm, home of Captain James Pendleton of the Continental Army and Governor of Virginia. In early June 1863 Pickett's Division deployed here to meet converging Federal threats on Lee's east flank. This was the last tactical action of this Division before Gettysburg. Grant's forces moved through here in the campaign of 1864 and later Sheridan's Calvary Corps of the Union Army. It is now **a national historic district with 22 buildings, a frame grocery store and a family cemetery. kingandqueenco.net**

KING GEORGE COUNTY

King George County was formed from Richmond County in 1720. It is named for King George I of Great Britain. It was reshaped along with Stafford and Westmoreland Counties in 1776 and 1777 to form the modern boundaries. The county seat is King George.

 ## WHERE TO START

FAMILY RESEARCH

King George Historical Society: The Research Center Library includes a collection of books on local area histories and published genealogical information.

> **FIND IT: 9483 Kings Highway, King George, VA 22485**
> From I-95 North exit #104 onto VA-207 E. In about 30 miles, continue on VA-207 E to Bowling Green bypass. In About 3 miles the bypass becomes A P Hill Blvd/ US-301 N. In about 17 miles turn left onto VA-3 W/Kings Highway. The Historical Society is inside the east end of the King George Courthouse. **(540) 775.9477   kghistory.org**

Central Rappahannock Heritage Center: The Central Rappahannock Heritage Center has more than 120,000 items of information dating back to the early 1700s. The Center includes information from the counties of **King George, Caroline, Spotsylvania, and Stafford, as well as the city of Fredericksburg.**

> **FIND IT: Central Rappahannock Heritage Center, 900 Barton St. #111, Fredericksburg, VA 22401** From Richmond, drive north on I-95 to exit # 130A and merge onto VA-3/E William Street. In about 1 mile turn left onto William Street. In one more mile turn right onto Barton Street. The Center is ahead on the right. **(540) 373.3704   crhcarchives.org**

The **Northern Neck of VA Historical Society**: The Society's library collection includes vital records, family histories, church and cemetery guides, histories of Virginia and Northern Neck towns and counties, immigration lists, census records, microfilm of the Northern Neck News, 1879-1939, and microfilm of the Virginia Citizen of Irvington, 1891-1917.

> **FIND IT: 15825 Kings Hwy, Montross, Virginia 22520**. From Richmond take I-64 East to exit 192 and merge onto US-360 E. Go about 43 miles and turn right onto US-360 E/Queen Street. Go about 7 miles and turn left onto Main Street. In less than a mile turn left onto VA-3. In about 11 miles watch for the Society on the right. There is plenty of parking in the front.
> **(804) 493.1862   nnvhs.org**

ORIGINAL DOCUMENTS

King George County Clerk of the Circuit Court has land and probate records from 1721.

> **FIND IT: 9483 Kings Highway, King George, VA 22485**
> Follow the above directions to the
> King George Historical Society.   **(540) 775.3322**

GOOD TO KNOW

James Madison, the fourth President of the United States, was born in Port Conway in southern King George County at **Belle Grove plantation.**

George Washington grew up in **Ferry Farm** and had many connections to King George County. He often visited his brother Samuel Washington of Choptank. He attended church at **St. Pauls Parish** on several occasions. The will of Augustine Washington, father of the first president, is recorded in King George County Courthouse.

KING WILLIAM COUNTY

King William County was formed in 1701 from King and Queen County. The county is named for William of Orange, King of England. The county seat is King William.

 **WHERE TO START**

FAMILY RESEARCH
The West Point Branch Library, 721 Main Street, West Point, VA 23181 has some genealogy files but the libraries in nearby Hanover County have major genealogy holdings. (804) 843.3244

Hanover Branch Library has a Virginiana Section that contains family files and other reference materials.

> **FIND IT: 7527 Library Drive, Hanover, VA 23060**
> From I-95 N exit #92 (Rt. 54 East) towards Hanover. Travel approximately 7 miles to the intersection with US-301. Turn right onto US-301. Travel about ½ mile and turn left onto Library Drive. The Library is ahead on the right.
> **(804) 365.6210   pamunkeylibrary.org**

ORIGINAL DOCUMENTS

King William County Clerk of the Circuit Court has deeds, wills, and court records from 1701.

> **FIND IT: Suite 130, 351 Courthouse Road, King William, VA 23086** From the Hanover Library turn right onto US-301 N. In about 5 miles turn right onto Rte. 651 and right again onto VA-30 E. In about 23 miles turn left onto Rte. 619 and right again onto Courthouse Road. Keep along this road until you see the new Courthouse out on your left. Enter under the arches through security. **(804) 769.4936**

GOOD TO KNOW

The 1725 Courthouse is the oldest courthouse in continuous use in the United States.

Chelsea Plantation, 874 Chelsea Plantation Lane, West Point, VA 23181. This 1709 plantation is the 2nd oldest that is open for tours. General Lafayette used the manor house for his headquarters and Robert E. Lee's grandmother was born and married here. **(804) 843.2386   virginia.org**

King William Historical Society and Museum at King William Courthouse. 227 Horse Landing Road, King William, VA 23086 The museum tells the history of King William County, VA. There are life size figures of individual important people. The story of the Pamunkey Indians is a significant portion of the museum. The museum is located inside the 1725 Courthouse complex very near the new Courthouse. **804.769.9619   kingwilliamhistory.org**

Mattaponi Reservation and Museum, Rte 2, West Point, VA 23181. A visit to the Mattaponi Reservation and Museum will provide a wonderful sense of the Mattaponi people. Some of the artifacts date back more than 1,000 years. A necklace that belonged to Pocahontas is on display.   **mattaponiindianmuseum.org**

Old St. John's Church, 103 St. John's Church Lane, West Point, VA 23181. This church has been restored to its original exterior appearance in 1734.   **oldstjohns.org**

Pamunkey Indian Tribe Museum, 175 Lay Landing Road, King William, VA, 23086. Located in King William on the Pamunkey Indian Reservation, this museum is a "living memory of Powhatan's People." Watch pottery being made using original techniques passed down from the generations.   **(804) 843.4792**

LANCASTER COUNTY

Lancaster County was established in 1651 from Northumberland and York counties. It was named for Lancaster in the United Kingdom. The county seat is Lancaster.

 **WHERE TO START**

FAMILY RESEARCH

Mary Ball Washington Museum & Library is an extensive historical and genealogical library with the main emphasis on Lancaster, Northumberland, Richmond, Westmoreland, Middlesex and Essex Counties.

> **FIND IT: 8346 Mary Ball Road, Lancaster, VA 22503** For the most direct route from Richmond travel east on I-64 E toward Norfolk and exit #192 onto US-360 E. In about 44 miles turn right onto US-360 E/Queen Street. In about 7 miles turn right onto VA-3 E. In about 23 miles the Museum and Library is ahead on the right. Park across the street.
> **(804) 462.7280   mbwm.org**

The **Northern Neck of Virginia Historical Society** library collection includes vital records, family histories, church and cemetery guides, histories of Virginia and Northern Neck towns and counties.

> **FIND IT: 15482 Kings Hwy, Montross, Virginia 22520**. From Richmond take I-64 East to exit #192 and merge onto US-360 E. In about 44 miles turn right onto US-360 E/Queen Street. In about 4 miles turn left onto Rte. 624. In less than 1 mile turn right onto Rte. 621. In about 2 miles turn left onto Rte. 690. In about 2 ½ miles turn left to stay on Rte. 690. In about 4 miles turn left onto VA-3 W. The Society is about 4 miles ahead on the left. Watch for the White sign in the front yard.
> **(804) 493.1862   nnvhs.org**

ORIGINAL DOCUMENTS

Lancaster County Clerk of the Circuit Court has most of the court records from 1652. The marriage records begin in 1701.

> **FIND IT: 8311 Mary Ball Road, Lancaster, VA 22503** From the Museum and Library continue on Mary Ball Road just past the Old Courthouse and turn right to drive back to the new Court complex behind it. Enter through security in the front. **(804) 462.5611**

GOOD TO KNOW

Lancaster County is the most densely populated county in the Northern Neck. Lancaster County's largest town is Kilmarnock.

Belle Isle State Park   1632 Belle Isle Road, Lancaster, VA

Christ Church. 420 Christ Church Rd, Weems, VA 22576
Completed in 1735, this Virginia historical landmark is the best preserved of Colonial Virginia's Anglican parish churches. The Christ Church features include a history of the church and Robert "King" Carter.
(804) 438.6855   christchurch1735.org

Kilmarnock Museum, 76 N Main Street, Kilmarnock, VA 22482
Steamboat Era Museum 156 King Carter Dr. Irvington, VA 22480
A collection of dioramas, artifacts, models, paintings, photos and a gift shop. **(804) 438.6888   steamboateramuseum.org**

Morattico Waterfront Museum, 6584 Morattico Road, Morattico, VA 22523 Artifacts, photos, and documents related to activities in a working watermen's settlement and the function of the general store are being preserved to honor the past and educate new generations.
(804) 462.0532   morattico.org

LEE COUNTY

Lee is the westernmost county in Virginia. It was formed in 1793 from Russell County. It was named for Light Horse Harry Lee, Governor of Virginia from 1791 to 1794. The county seat is Jonesville.

 ## WHERE TO START

FAMILY RESEARCH

Lee County Library: For an overview of all Lee County records and a look at records that have been transcribed, go first to the Lee County library in Pennington Gap, VA.

> **FIND IT: 539 Joslyn Avenue, Pennington Gap, VA 24277.** From I-81 S exit 1B toward Gate City, VA. Follow it around onto US-58/Gate City Hwy. In about 24 miles turn right onto Wadlow Gap Hwy/ VA-224N and then right onto US-23N. In about 18 miles turn left onto Duff Patt Hwy/US-58. Go about 11 miles and bear right onto Woodway Road. In about 5 miles turn left onto E Morgan Ave/US-58 ALT. In about ½ mile turn left onto Joslyn Ave. The library is ahead on the right behind the Farmers and Miners Bank. **(276) 546.1141   lprlibrary.org**

Lee County Historical and Genealogical Society: An appointment is necessary for research. Their website lists the resources available.

> **FIND IT:** Lee County Historical and Genealogical Society, Jonesville, VA 24263. **(276) 346.1030   leecountyhistoricalsociety.org**

ORIGINAL DOCUMENTS

Lee County Clerk of the Circuit Court Office has produced a brochure that will explain what records are there and how to access them.

> **FIND IT: 33640 Main Street, Jonesville, VA 24263.** From the library go back to E Morgan Ave/US-58Alt and turn left. In about 8 miles, this road will become Main Street in the town of Jonesville, VA. The Courthouse is ahead on the left at the intersection of Main and Church Streets. Turn left to park on Church Street and enter through the side entrance. The Clerk's Office is straight ahead. **(276) 346.7763**

GOOD TO KNOW

The Cumberland Gap, a passage through the Appalachian Mountains is at Lee County's western tip. **Wilderness Road** was carved by Daniel Boone in 1775 to open America's first western frontier. **Wilderness Road State Park** is in Ewing, VA about 50 miles south of Jonesville which leads to **Cumberland Gap State Park** just across the state line in Kentucky.

The Trail of the Lonesome Pine State Outdoor Drama
Based on a novel by John Fox, Jr., **The Trail of The Lonesome Pine** is a musical drama that (to quote the brochure) "depicts the story of when the discovery of coal and iron ore forced the lusty, proud mountain people into making many drastic changes in their way of life."
**518 Clinton Ave. E, Big Stone Gap, Virginia
(276) 523.1235   trailofthelonesomepine.com**

LOUDOUN COUNTY

Loudoun County was formed in 1757 from Fairfax County. The county is named for John Campbell, Fourth Earl of Loudoun and Governor of Virginia from 1756–59. The county seat is Leesburg.

 **WHERE TO START**

FAMILY RESEARCH

Thomas Balch Library is a history and genealogy library with focus on Loudoun County, regional and Virginia history. It is designated as an Underground Railroad research site.

> **FIND IT: 208 W Market Street, Leesburg, VA 20176** From Richmond follow I-95 N to exit 152B toward Manassas. Merge onto VA-234/Dumfries Road. Go about 14 miles and turn right onto VA-294/Prince William Pkwy. In about 4 miles stay straight. Road name changes to Liberia Ave. In about 2 miles turn right onto VA-28N/ Centerville Road. In about 20 miles exit left at the fork and follow signs to VA-7 W and merge onto Harry Byrd Hwy toward Leesburg. In about 7 miles continue on this road now called E Market. In about 1 mile turn left to stay on E Market Street. When you cross Liberty Street, watch for the driveway just ahead on the right. Park in the back. (East becomes West Market at King Street). **(703) 737.7195**

ORIGINAL DOCUMENTS

Loudoun County Circuit Court Archives: Loudoun County is fortunate to have all its original records that date back to 1757. Plan to stay awhile.

FIND IT: 18 E Market Street, Leesburg, VA 20176. There are 2 free parking lots fairly close to the Archives Building on the Courthouse Green. From the driveway of the Balch Library turn left back onto W Market Street. Continue on past the Courthouse and take the first left onto Church Street. There is a prominent sign for public parking at this intersection. Just follow the signs to one of two lots in that direction. Each parking lot has signs with a map of the area around the Courthouse. Walk back up Church Street, turn right on Market Street and enter the new courthouse directly across from the post office through court security. Take the elevator up (or walk) to the Circuit Court Clerk's Office on the 3rd floor and turn left. Go through the Clerk's Office down a hallway and through another door to another elevator. Take this one down to B2. The entrance to historic records is on your right when you exit the elevator.
(703) 737.8775   loudoun.gov/clerk

GOOD TO KNOW

Oatlands Historic House and Gardens was formed in 1798. By 1860, the enslaved community here numbered 132 men, women and children. **20850 Oatlands Plantation Lane · Leesburg, VA 20175 (703) 777.3174   oatlands.org**

The Davis Mansion began as a small fieldstone house, built in about 1780 and expanded upon through the following decades until it became the 22-room Greek Revival estate of today.
17263 Southern Planter Ln., Leesburg, VA 20176 (703) 777.2414

Middleburg is a small, designated historic village in Loudoun County. The oldest building in town is the Red Fox Inn originally established in 1728. Also of note is the **National Sporting Library & Museum, 102 The Plains Rd, Middleburg, VA 20118 (540) 687.6542   visitloudoun.org**

LOUISA COUNTY

Louisa County was created in 1742 from Hanover County. It was named in honor of the youngest daughter of King George II. The county seat is Louisa.

 **WHERE TO START**

FAMILY RESEARCH

Jefferson-Madison Regional Library's Genealogy Research Room has a copy of every book published for Louisa County research. The room contains numerous volumes on surrounding counties and Virginia history. Ask for a key to the room.

> **FIND IT: 881 Davis Hwy., Mineral, VA 23117.** From Richmond follow I-64 W to exit 159 and turn right onto US-522 N. In about 15 miles US-522 merges with US-33 in Cuckoo, VA. Turn left and take a right in about 1/3 mile to stay on 522 N. In about 4 miles stay straight ahead through the traffic light in the town of Mineral. This road becomes VA-22 W/ Piedmont Avenue. The Library is ahead on the left just past the Louisa County High School. Turn left onto Hwy 778 and then an immediate right into the parking lot. **(540) 894.5853**

The Louisa County Historical Society at the Sargeant Museum's archives consist of family files, documents, and photographs. An appointment is necessary for research. Extensive on-line resources are available at **piedmontvahistory.org** and **trevilians.com.**

> **FIND IT: 214 Fredericksburg Avenue, Louisa, VA 23093** From the Library turn left onto VA-22 W. In about 5 miles this road becomes Main Street in the town of Louisa. Turn right at a traffic light onto Fredericksburg Avenue at the Ford Dealer. The Museum is the second left and then an immediate right

into the Arts Center parking. Go straight ahead to parking
for the Museum. **(540) 967.5975 louisahistory.org**

ORIGINAL DOCUMENTS

Louisa County Clerk of the Circuit Court has all deeds, wills
and marriages in a well-organized record room.

> **FIND IT: 100 W. Main Street, Louisa, VA 23093**   From the
> Museum go back out of the parking lot turn right and right again
> at the light onto W Main Street. The Courthouse is ahead on the
> left. The front entrance to the Courthouse is no longer in use.
> Street parking is available on either side and behind the building.
> Enter through security at the rear entrance. The Record room is
> all on one floor in the room to your left.

GOOD TO KNOW

visitlouisa.com to download a visitor guide.

Green Springs National Historic Landmark District is a 14,000 acre
agricultural landscape. Thirty-five homes and buildings in the District
are listed on the National Register of Historic Places. 8,000 acres are held
in conservation/preservation easements by the National Park Service,
Virginia Department of Historic Resources and Historic Green Springs,
Inc. A brochure on the district is available at **nps.gov/grsp/index**

The Battlefield of Trevilian Station, is the site of the largest all cavalry
action of the Civil War. Visit **trevilianstation.org** for more information
and to download a map for a driving tour. Get an on-line story map of
the battlefield tour at **louisahistory.org**

LUNENBURG COUNTY

Lunenburg County was formed from Brunswick County in 1746. The county is named for the former Duchy of Brunswick-Luneburg in Germany. The county seat is now spelled Lunenburg.

 **WHERE TO START**

FAMILY RESEARCH

Victoria Public Library Genealogy Resource Room: This is the best place to begin. Ask at the desk to be admitted to the Resource Room. Someone will help you get started. Here you can access an index to family files in the two other libraries in Lunenburg County.

> **FIND IT: 11435 Courthouse Road, Victoria, VA 23974**
> From Richmond make your way south to US-360 W: west on I-64, south on VA-288 and merge onto US-360 W toward Amelia. In about 39 miles turn left onto State Rte 723. In about 13 miles turn right onto VA-49 S/Falls Road. This becomes Nottoway Blvd. Continue on around until this road becomes Main Street then turn left onto 7th Street/Courthouse Road. The Library is just ahead on the right. Watch for a row of white buildings along the sidewalk. Park on the street.
> **(434) 696.3416   lunenburglibraries.org**

ORIGINAL DOCUMENTS

Lunenburg County Clerk of the Circuit Court has complete court records from 1746.

> **FIND IT: 11435 Courthouse Road, Lunenburg, VA 23952**
> From the Victoria Library go back along 7th Street and turn right. Go one block and turn left onto Court Street. Follow this road

for about 3 miles. The Courthouse will be on the right. Park on the street. To enter the Clerk's Office, from the front of the Courthouse walk down the left side of the building to the 3rd entrance. **(434) 696.2132**

GOOD TO KNOW

The **Fifth Avenue Historic District** is a national historic district located at Kenbridge, Virginia. The dwellings were constructed between 1890 and 1930. Notable non-residential buildings include the Harris Hospital (c. 1910), Kenbridge Baptist Church (1948), Kenbridge Methodist Church (1914), and Kenbridge High School (1921), designed by noted Richmond architect Charles M. Robinson.

Spring Bank, also known as Ravenscroft and Magnolia Grove, is a privately owned historic plantation home located near Lunenburg, Virginia. It was built about 1793. On the property are the smokehouse, a log slave quarter, and frame tobacco barn, and the remains of dependencies, including a kitchen/laundry, ice house, spring house, and a dam. Also located on the property are a family cemetery and two other burial grounds.

Lunenburg Courthouse Historic District includes the courthouse built in 1827. Associated with the courthouse is a large, hipped-roofed frame house which was once a tavern. The Law Offices have recently been restored by the Lunenburg Historical Society.

Flat Rock is a historic tobacco plantation home and farm located near Kenbridge, Virginia. It was built about 1846, but has a rear ell dated to about 1835. Original weatherboard and a side gable roof are still present. The site is privately owned.

Brickland is a historic plantation home located near Kenbridge, Virginia. The original section was built about 1818, with an addition built about 1822, and rear addition in 1920. Also on the property are a pump house, smokehouse, Lunenburg County's first post office, a summer kitchen, the ruins of slave quarters and an ice house. It is privately owned.

MADISON COUNTY

Madison County was formed in 1793 from Orange County. The county is named for the Madison family that owned land along the Rapidan River. President James Madison is a descendant of that family. The county seat is Madison.

WHERE TO START

FAMILY RESEARCH

Madison County Library is also known as the Thomas W. Lewis House. Built in 1852 it served as a home for the Lewis family, as well as a Methodist Parsonage. In 1967 it was renovated to serve as the county's library.

> **FIND IT: 402 N. Main Street, Madison, VA 22727**
> From Richmond take I-64 West about 54 miles to exit 136. Turn right onto US-15N/US-33. In about 12 miles at the traffic circle take the second exit to stay on US-33 and turn right onto VA-231N. Go about 16 miles and turn left onto VA- 230W. In ½ mile merge/turn right onto US-29. IN about 1 mile bear left onto US-29Bus. This becomes South and then North Main Street. Continue on past the Courthouse to the Library on the right. Watch for the signs as the building sits way back off the road.
> **(540) 948.4720   madisoncountyvalibrary.org**

Madison County Historical Society has a research room which contains a collection of genealogies of Madison families, histories and pictures of old Madison County churches, schools, and other buildings.

> **FIND IT: 124 N. Main Street, Madison, VA 22727** From the Library turn left onto Main Street and continue along to the Historical Society on the left.
> **(540) 948.5488   madisonvahistoricalsociety.org**

ORIGINAL DOCUMENTS

Madison County Clerk of the Circuit Court has marriage, divorce, probate, court and land records from 1793 in the record room.

> FIND IT: 1 **South Main Street, Madison, VA 22727** From the Library or the Historical Society, turn back left onto North Main Street and follow it back to the Courthouse. There is a sign for the Clerk's Office in front of the building. Park in the lot to the right. **(540) 948.6888**

GOOD TO KNOW

The town of Madison has produced an excellent guide to Downtown Madison. Get a copy of the map from the **Visitor Center at 110A ZN. Main Street in Madison. (540) 948.4455**

The Old Rag Mountain hike in the Shenandoah National Park is one of the most popular hikes in the mid-Atlantic region. With many spectacular panoramic views, and one of the most challenging rock scrambles in the park, this circuit hike is a favorite of many hikers. But be prepared for the crowds.

Graves Mountain Lodge Apple Harvest Festival. Enjoy fun-filled days complete with Graves famous Food, live Bluegrass Music & Cloggers, Arts & Crafts, Hay Maze & Hay Mountain, Hayrides, Horseback Rides, Pick your own apples, tour the family's working educational farm, visit the animals and more. Experience farm days of yesteryear, watch kettles of apple butter cook over an open fire. **gravesmountain.com**

MATHEWS COUNTY

Mathews County was formed in 1791 from part of Gloucester County. The county was named for Brigadier General Thomas Mathews, then speaker of the House of Delegates of the General Assembly of Virginia. The county seat is Mathews.

 ## WHERE TO START

FAMILY RESEARCH

The **Mathews Memorial Library** houses collections in the Chesapeake Room and the Herman Hollerith Archival Room in partnership with the Mathews County Historical Society.

> **FIND IT: 251 Main Street, Mathews Virginia 23109** From Richmond follow I-64 E for about 30 miles. Exit 220 onto VA-33 E/Eltham Road and go about 20 miles. At a traffic light, this road becomes VA-198 E/Glenn's Road. Go about 5 more miles and turn left to stay on VA-198 E. In about 18 miles turn right onto VA-14 E. The library is ahead on the left. It is a white stone building with imbedded columns. Park on the street.
> **(804) 725.5747   mathewslibrary.org**

ORIGINAL DOCUMENTS

Mathews County Clerk of the Circuit Court has records from 1865. Many of the early county records were destroyed during the American Civil War. The wills are indexed in the Grantor Deed Books but are bound into separate Will Books.

> **FIND IT: 10622 Buckley Hall Road, Mathews, VA 23109**
> From the Library go back along Main Street and turn left back onto Buckley Hall Road. The County Offices are about ½ mile ahead on the left. **(804) 725.2550**

GOOD TO KNOW

With only 94 square miles of land, Mathews is one of the smallest of Virginia's counties.

The Mathews County Visitor Center is in Sibley's General Store on Main Street in the heart of the village. **visitmathews.com**

Bethel Beach has 83 acres of natural habitat with dunes, tidal ponds and ultra wide views of the Chesapeake Bay.

William's Wharf Landing is the place to be for access to the East River. Three acres of waterfront open space with pier fishing, floating docks, shoreline walkways, an open-air pavilion, and viewing tower. Pavilion and facilities open to the public year round sunrise to sunset.

Sunset at New Point Preserve is favored by locals who gather with friends on the observation walkway for a perfect way to end the day.

The third oldest lighthouse on the Chesapeake Bay, **New Point Comfort Lighthouse** was commissioned in 1804 by Thomas Jefferson. The 55-foot octagonal sandstone lighthouse sits on an island, separated from the mainland by the Hurricane of 1933. Two public viewing areas provide excellent opportunities to get up close and personal with area wildlife and the natural shoreline of the Mobjack Bay.

Birding Trails: East River Trail; New Point Comfort Trail; Winter Harbor/Horn Harbor Trail; Gwynn's Island Trail; Piankatank River Trail. The Virginia counties of Charlotte, Bath, and Mathews are significant in that none of them have a traffic signal.

MECKLENBURG COUNTY

Mecklenburg County was formed in 1765 from Lunenburg County.
It was named after Queen Charlotte of Mecklenburg-Strelitz. The county
seat is Boydton.

 **WHERE TO START**

FAMILY RESEARCH

The local library is the best place to begin. There is a specific genealogy
section with a computer to search their catalogue. Heritage Quest and
some microfilm are also available.

> **FIND IT: Boydton Public Library, 1294 Jefferson Street,
> Boydton, VA 23917** From Richmond make your way south
> onto I-95 and then to I-85 S at exit #51. In about 55 miles exit
> #12 B toward South Hill, VA. Keep left and then turn right onto
> US-58 W. In about 17 miles turn left onto Washington Street/
> VA 92. Take the 3rd right onto Jefferson Street. The Library is at
> the corner of Jefferson and Washington Streets. There is plenty
> of street parking but some places in front of the library
> are reserved for the Sheriff's Office.
> **(434) 738.6580   youseemore.com/mecklib**

ORIGINAL DOCUMENTS

Mecklenburg County Clerk of the Circuit Court has most of
the records from 1765 available. The record room is a delightful place for
research. Check in with one of the deputy clerks when you enter.

> **FIND IT: 393 Washington Street, Boydton, VA 23917**
> The Courthouse is directly across Jefferson Street from the
> Library. Enter through security from the front, turn left and
> go through two sets of doors to enter the record room.
> **(434) 738.6191**

GOOD TO KNOW

Prestwould, **429 Prestwould Drive, Clarksville, VA 23927** is the most complete gentry home in Virginia. Built in 1794 by Sir Peyton Skipwith, originally of England and then Virginia, many of the original outbuildings and Lady Jean's Garden remain. The site has one of the largest collections of slave writings in the country.
(804) 374.8672 **www.aaheritageva.org**

MacCallum More Gardens and Museum, **603 Hudgins Street, Chase City, VA 23924** MacCallum More, Scottish for Home of the Clan, was begun in 1929 by Lucy M. Hudgins, wife of Edward W. Hudgins, former Chief Justice of the Virginia Supreme Court of Appeals. The gardens feature an arboretum, herb, wildflower, rose and theme gardens, as well as, fountains and eclectic imported works of art. The museum has permanent exhibits. **(434) 372.0502** **mmmg.org**

There are three notable museums in South Hill, VA.:

The Tobacco Farm Life Museum of Virginia, 306 W Main Street

Model Railroad Museum and Wildlife exhibit, 201 S. Mecklenburg Ave

Virginia S. Evans Doll Museum, 201 S Mecklenburg Ave.

Find more information at **southhillva.org**

Buggs Island Lake, Lake Gaston, and Lake Gordon are excellent sites for fishing and water sports.

MIDDLESEX COUNTY

Middlesex County was formed from Lancaster County in 1673. It was most likely named for the English county of the same name. The county seat is Saluda.

 **WHERE TO START**

FAMILY RESEARCH

Middlesex County Museum and Historical Society has a large collection of reference books for families and homesteads presently or formerly in the county. Someone will guide you to various plats, historical births, christenings, baptisms, marriages, deaths and burials. The Museum's staff is experienced in research and can point you in the correct direction. **The Main Museum** has an extensive collection that covers from ancient times to Desert Storm. Exhibits include Fossils, Native American artifacts, Historic Maps, Childhood in Middlesex, Veterans (including Chesty Puller), Social Life, and a 1920's General Store. **The Clerk's Office Exhibit** (on the grounds of the historic courthouse) has themes pulled from historical documents County Clerk P.T. Woodward hid in 1863 during the Union troops' visit to Saluda. **(804) 758.3663 middlesexmuseum.com**

> **FIND IT: 777 General Puller Hwy, Saluda. VA 23149** From Richmond travel east on I-64 E. In about 30 miles exit #220 and merge onto VA-33 toward West Point. In about 19 miles turn left onto US-17 N/VA-33 E. In about 2 miles bear slight right onto US-17Bus. In about 1 mile turn left onto VA-33E. The Middlesex County Museum is the second building on the right.

ORIGINAL DOCUMENTS

Middlesex County Clerk of the Circuit Court has court, will and deed records dating from 1673 to present.

FIND IT: 877 General Puller Hwy, Saluda, VA 23149 From the museum, head east one block to the traffic light in front of the historic courthouse. Go through the light and take the first left just past the historic courthouse. The new courthouse sits behind the old courthouse. The Record Room is on the second floor. There is ample parking. **(804) 758.5317**

Mary Ball Washington Museum & Library is an extensive genealogical library with the main emphasis on Lancaster, Northumberland, Richmond, Westmoreland, Middlesex and Essex Counties. See Lancaster County for directions.

GOOD TO KNOW

Middlesex County Tourism
visitmiddlesexva.org

Deltaville Maritime Museum, 287 Jackson Creek Road, Deltaville, VA 23043. **(804) 776.7200** **deltavillemuseum.com**

Hewick Plantation, 5123 Old Virginia Street, Urbanna, Virginia 23175 was a gathering place for many of the important families of Virginia. The plantation house is currently undergoing an extensive restoration. **(804) 758.1678** **hewickplantation.com**

Wilton House, 1425 Twiggs Ferry Rd., Hartfield, VA 23071 a superbly preserved 1763 plantation house. Wilton House was the seat of the Churchill family along the southern end of Middlesex County. **(804) 824.3038** **wiltonhousevirginia.org**

MONTGOMERY COUNTY

Montgomery County was formed from Fincastle and Botetourt Counties in 1773. It was named after Revolutionary War Brigadier-General Richard Montgomery. The county seat is Christiansburg.

 WHERE TO START

FAMILY RESEARCH

Montgomery Museum and Lewis Regional Art Center:
Onsite Reference Library and genealogy files.

> FIND IT: **300 Pepper St, SE Christiansburg, VA 24073**
> Follow I-64 West to I-81 South. Exit 118 C-B-A toward Christiansburg then keep left onto exit B toward US 460/Blacksburg. In about 1 mile turn left onto US-460 Bus/Christiansburg. In about 2 miles turn left onto 1ˢᵗ Street and take the first left onto Pepper Street. Library and Museum house is ahead on the left. There is a small sign in the front and a handicapped ramp to the front door.
> **(540) 382.5644   montgomerymuseum.org**

ORIGINAL DOCUMENTS

Montgomery County Clerk of the Circuit Court has all Deeds and Wills from 1773. Marriage records begin in 1777. Show a photo ID to request a swipe card for access to the historic records room.

> FIND IT: **55 East Main Street, Christiansburg, VA**
> From the Museum go back down Pepper Street. Just before the traffic light and just past the large red brick building on your left, is the parking lot for the Courthouse. Park here and once on foot, turn left at the light and left again to enter the building from East Main Street. The Clerk's Office occupies the first floor.
> **(540) 382.5760**

GOOD TO KNOW

The Yellow Sulphur Spring, currently flowing out of a well under a Gazebo, is a cold mineral spring rich in calcium, magnesium, iron, copper and sulfate. The standing hotel was begun in 1810 and row cottages were constructed during the 1840's.
yellowsulphursprings.com

Established in 1792, **Historic Christiansburg** includes: **Christiansburg Industrial Institute** (140 Scattergood Dr.), a private primary school for African-Americans established in 1866 and once supervised by Booker T. Washington. Three buildings remain; one is now a museum. Cambria Historic District (500 Depot St.). Includes a railroad depot museum, collectibles/antique shop and specialty shops.
christiansburginstitute.org

Smithfield is a plantation outside Blacksburg, VA built from 1772 to 1774 as a home by Col. William Preston. It was the birthplace of two Virginia Governors: James Patton Preston and John B. Floyd. The property has been restored and is open to the public.
smithfieldplantation.org

Local History and Genealogical Research in the University Libraries, Virginia Tech University, Blacksburg, VA: download this 20+ page guide from the library website **lib.vt.edu**. This is a guide to the resources including family files and will be a great help with Southwest Virginia research.

NELSON COUNTY

Nelson County was formed from Amherst County in 1807. The county is named for Virginia Governor Thomas Nelson, a signer of the Declaration of Independence. The county seat is Lovingston.

 WHERE TO START

FAMILY RESEARCH

The Nelson Memorial Library is the best place to begin. A collection of local history materials and cemetery records is maintained by the **Nelson County Historical Society**. The **Nelson County Visitor Center** is located on the lower level of the library.

> **FIND IT: 8519 Thomas Nelson Hwy, Lovingston, VA 22949**
> Take I-64 West from Richmond and continue to Charlottesville. Exit #118A onto Hwy 29 South. Stay on Hwy 29 for about 30 miles to Lovingston. The Visitors Center, and Library are on the right side of the highway just 2/10 mile south of the Lovingston traffic light. The building is up on slight hill. There is plenty of parking. **(434) 263.5904   jmrl.org**

ORIGINAL DOCUMENTS

Nelson County Clerk of the Circuit Court: The Clerk's Office and Record Room are on the first floor of the Courthouse. Ask about the unique chart for grantors and grantees.

> **FIND IT: 84 Courthouse Square, Lovingston, VA 22949**
> From the Library head back into town on VA-29 and keep right onto VA-29 Bus. Turn right on to VA-1002, cross Court Street and follow signs to the Courthouse. **(434) 263.7020**

GOOD TO KNOW

Return to Walton's Mountain 6484 Rockfish River Road, Schuyler, VA 22969. Step back in time and memory to John-Boy's bedroom, the Waltons' kitchen and living room and Ike Godsey's store, which also serves as the museum's gift shop; (434) 831.2000 *waltonmuseum.org*

Oakland-Nelson County Museum of History, 5365 Thomas Nelson Hwy, Arrington, VA 22922 is a ca. 1840s Tavern. Exhibits include Hurricane Camille and its Aftermath. And "Cuttin' On The Lights": How the lives of rural people changes when electricity came to Nelson County in the 1930s, featuring early appliances and oral histories. **(434) 263.8400   oakland-museum.org**

Crabtree Falls, 11581 Crabtree Falls Hwy, Montebello, VA 24464 Visit the highest cascading waterfall east of the Mississippi- –a series of five major cascades that fall a total distance of 1,200 feet. The first overlook is just 700 feet from the new lower parking lot. **nelsoncounty-va.gov/tourism**

Wintergreen Resort, Rte. 664, Wintergreen, VA 22958 is a four season resort offering skiing, golf, tennis, and many hiking trails near the Blue Ridge Parkway and Ravens Roost Overlook. **(434) 325.2200   wintergreenresort.com**

Rockfish Valley Foundation: A community volunteer based organization supporting the Rockfish River trails, Rockfish Valley Foundation Natural History Center, Nelson Scenic Loop, and Spruce Creek Park. **rockfishvalley.org**

NEW KENT COUNTY

New Kent County was formed in 1654 from York County. The county's name originated because several prominent inhabitants had been forced from their settlement at Kent Island, Maryland by Lord Baltimore when the state of Maryland was formed. The county seat is New Kent.

 **WHERE TO START**

FAMILY RESEARCH

The public library in New Kent is a good place to start. The Genealogy Reference area provides access to electronic databases as well as many books for research.

> **FIND IT: Heritage Public Library 6215 D Chesapeake Circle, New Kent, VA 23124**   From Richmond follow I-64 E toward Virginia Beach. In about 24 miles exit #214. Follow the ramp and turn right onto VA-155 S/ Courthouse Road. In .3 mile turn right onto Cheaspeake Circle. Keep right and then turn right to stay on this road. It will end in the parking lot for the Library on your left. **(804) 966.2480   heritagepubliclibrary.org**

The Old Jail is open for genealogy research every Monday except holidays, from 10:00 - 2:00.

> **FIND IT: The Old Jail, 12007 Courthouse Cir, New Kent, VA 23124** From the library go back to Courthouse Road and turn left. In about 2 ½ miles turn right onto VA-249 E/New Kent Hwy. In about 2 miles turn right onto Courthouse Cir. Drive along in front of the Courthouse to the parking lot on the left. **(804) 510.3826   lavonne@newkenthistoricalsoc.com**

ORIGINAL DOCUMENTS

New Kent County Clerk of the Circuit Court has records from 1865. The county has suffered major record loss. Be sure to ask about the "Chandler Book" for research.

> **FIND IT: 12001 Courthouse Circle, New Kent, VA 23124.**
> From the Old Jail walk across the square to the Courthouse.
> Enter through security. **(804) 966.9520**

GOOD TO KNOW

St. Peter's Church, 8400 St. Peters Ln, New Kent, VA 23124, the "First Church of the First First-Lady" was established on April 29, 1678. In January 1759 Col. George Washington and Martha Dandridge Curtis were married there. The original portion of St. Peter's Parish Church is one of the few Jacobean structures in America. Its 1740 stump tower is also rare. **(804) 932.4846   stpetersnewkent.org**

Wahrani Nature Park is a bird-watcher's paradise. There are trails through old growth trees "to a sweeping overlook and a pair of colonial graves." **visitnewkent.com**

New Kent is the first county in Virginia to have fully mapped and signed **bicycle routes**. These bike routes, ranging from 15- to 100-miles, start and end at the New Kent Visitors and Commerce Center on Vineyards Parkway at I-64 Exit 214. Bike route maps as well as information about the Nature Park can be downloaded from **visitnewkent.com**

NORTHAMPTON COUNTY

Accomac Shire was established by the House of Burgesses in 1634 as one of the original eight shires of Virginia. In 1642 the county name was changed to Northampton, most likely for Northamptonshire in England. Northampton was then split into two counties in 1663. The southern area remained as Northampton County. The county seat is Eastville.

WHERE TO START

FAMILY RESEARCH

On the Eastern Shore, the researcher is directed to the town of Accomac in Accomack County to begin.

Eastern Shore Public Library: The researcher will find a large collection of primary and secondary sources. Genealogical files include those of Mark C. Lewis, Stratton Nottingham, Nora M. Turman, and E. Spenser Wise. The Miles files and the Mears Collection are available through the library's website. See Accomack County for directions.

ORIGINAL DOCUMENTS

Northampton County Clerk of the Circuit Court has continuous court records that exist from 1632.

> **FIND IT: 16404 Courthouse Rd, Eastville, VA 23347** From the Eastern Shore Library, travel south on US-13 about 28 miles. Bear right onto US Bus/ Courthouse Road. In about one mile, just past the intersection with Willow Oak Road, and on the right (west) side of the road, stands the 1899 Courthouse. The new County Court Complex is behind this building. There is plenty of parking. Enter through security in the front and ask for directions to the Record Room. The Clerk of the Court has complied a wonderful book about the records in Northampton County. It is free to the researcher. **(757) 678.0440**

GOOD TO KNOW

10 miles north of the Bay Tunnel on the Eastern Shore is the town of
Cape Charles, VA. The Historical Society of Cape Charles maintains
a museum with a rich collection of early postcards, photographs,
timetables, documents, and objects which details the beginnings
of **Cape Charles** in the 1880s. **Take U.S. 13 and follow signs
to Cape Charles, located about 10 miles north of the entrance (exit)
to the Chesapeake Bay Bridge Tunnel. Go west on State Route 184.**
(757) 331.1008   smallmuseum.org/capechas

Chincoteague, and **Assateague** Islands are just north of Accomac.
Wallops Flight Facility, **a** NASA space launch base, is located at
Chincoteague. **Tangier Island,** and **Smith Island**, off the western shore in
the Chesapeake Bay, are additional destinations reached by daily ferries.

**Blackwater Wildlife Refuge 2145 Key Wallace Drive, Cambridge,
Md 21613** If you have a passion for birding and wildlife, a two hour
drive into Maryland from Accomac will be worth the effort. A beautiful
Visitor Center, a Wildlife Drive, hiking trails, paddling trails, and miles of
cycling roads can be found here. The Refuge is unique in that it hosts the
largest remaining natural population of Delmarva fox squirrels and is also
host to the largest breeding population of bald eagles on the East Coast,
north of Florida. **(410) 228.2677   fws.gov/blackwater**

NORTHUMBERLAND COUNTY

In 1634 when the eight shires of the Virginia Colony were formed the area that is now Northumberland County was Chickacoan, an Indian Territory. By 1648 the county was officially organized and named for County Northumberland, England. The county seat is Heathsville.

WHERE TO START

FAMILY RESEARCH

Northumberland County Historical Society is a well-organized history and genealogy research library. This is the best place to begin. It is in the basement level of the Ball Memorial Museum and Library Building. The new Courthouse is nearby.

> **FIND IT: 86 Back Street, Heathsville, VA 22473**. From Richmond follow I-64 E to US-360 E. Exit # 192 onto Mechanicsville Trpk. In about 41 miles keep left to stay on US-360 E. In about 3 more miles turn right to stay on US-360 E/Queen Street. In about 19 miles turn right to stay on US-360 E. In about 7 miles watch for a large white house and the EVB Bank sign. Turn right onto Rte. 1001 and make the next right back to a driveway for a brick house on the left. The library entrance is on the side. There a fee for research.
> **(804) 580.8581** **northumberlandhistoryva.org**

ORIGINAL DOCUMENTS

Northumberland County Clerk of the Circuit Court has a partial collection of records from 1647 to 1737. From the 1738 to the present most deeds and wills can be found. The 1661 register for St. Stephens Parish is here.

FIND IT: **220 Judicial Place, Heathsville, VA 22473** is on down Rte 1001 from the Society. **(804) 580.3700**

GOOD TO KNOW

The Reedville Fishermen's Museum, end of Hwy 360 in the historic town of Reedville, is an affiliate member of the Council of American Maritime Museums and dedicated to preserving the heritage of the maritime history of the lower Chesapeake Bay, the watermen who have made their living there and the menhaden industry that has existed in Reedville for over a century. Today Reedville is one of the major ports for the landing of commercial fish in the United States, second only to Kodiak, Alaska. **(804) 453.6529   rfmuseum.org**

The Northern Neck Farm Museum, 12705 Northumberland Hwy, Heathsville, VA 22473, began with a collector, an individual who refused to discard what was once considered useful and later became obsolete. Luther Welch, a native of Northumberland County, grew his collection of farm equipment and wanted to share it. Other farmers and community members shared his dream and a five county regional museum was formed in 2006 to tell the story of agriculture on the Northern Neck of Virginia. **(804) 761.5952   thefarmmuseum.org**

Rice's Hotel-Hughlett's Tavern, 73 Monument Pl., Heathsville, VA 22473 is the last surviving 1700s structure of its kind in the Northern Neck. The original three-room tavern was built by John Hughlett some 250 years ago, and is on both the Virginia and National Registers of Historic Places. The hotel is very near the Historical Society and just in front of the new Courts building. **(804) 580.3377**

NOTTOWAY COUNTY

First known as Nottoway Parish, a district of Amelia County, Nottoway Parish became Nottoway County in 1789. The name comes from Nadowa, an Algonquian word meaning rattlesnake. The county seat is Nottoway.

WHERE TO START

FAMILY RESEARCH

Crewe Library Family History Room: This is the best place to begin. The Historical Society for Nottoway County is still in transition and doesn't yet have a home.

> **FIND IT 400 Tyler Street, Crewe, VA 23930** From Richmond make your way south to US-360 W: west on I-64, south on VA-288 and merge onto US-360 W toward Amelia. In about 36 miles turn left onto State Rte 615/Mountain Hall Road. This road becomes Tyler Street/619. The Library is about 4 miles ahead on the left at the corner of Tyler and E Pennsylvania Ave. There is plenty of parking in front. **(434) 645.7527**

Lunenburg County Public Library: also called The Victoria Library, is a short drive from Crewe, VA. The genealogy room here is a good resource for Nottoway County family research. See Lunenburg County for directions.

ORIGINAL DOCUMENTS

Nottoway County Clerk of the Circuit Court has records from1865. The early records were burned in 1865.

> **FIND IT: 328 W Courthouse Rd, Crewe, VA 23955**. From the library turn back left onto Tyler Street. In about .3 mile turn left onto US-460 E. In about 4 miles exit onto US-460 Bus

ramp and turn right onto US-460Bus/Old Nottaway Road. Turn right onto W Court House Road. The Courthouse is ahead on the right. Park across the street. Follow the stone steps to a small brick building to the left of the Courthouse. This is the entrance to the Clerk's Office and Record Room. **(434) 645.9043**

GOOD TO KNOW

Crewe Railroad Museum 100 Virginia Ave, Crewe, VA 23930
Climb on a diesel engine, a caboose, and steam engine # 606. In the station, enjoy a room full of pictures and artifacts with their history.
(434) 645.9868

Schwartz Tavern 100 Tavern Street, Blackstone, VA 23824 The oldest building in Blackstone, the tavern's location dates to 1798. Each room in the tavern contains period pieces and tells the story of how a family might live. **(434) 292.7795**

Robert Thomas Carriage Museum 217 North High Street, Blackstone, VA 23824 Thirty-five horse drawn vehicles have been intricately restored The collection is displayed in a carriage house style setting complete with guides and interpretive signs that give a glimpse into the horse drawn era. **(434) 292.1459**

WSVS Radio Station 1032 Melody Lane, Crewe, VA 23930 The station that hosted some of the most famous American Roots musicians, including Flatt & Scruggs and the Foggy Mountain Boys has been restored and continues to host live music every Saturday at noon.
(434) 645.7743

ORANGE COUNTY

Orange County was formed in 1734 from Spotsylvania County. It is possible that Orange was once the largest county that ever existed. It was named for William III of England. The county seat is Orange.

 **WHERE TO START**

FAMILY RESEARCH

The Orange County Historical Society, Inc. is a research, archival, and educational organization. The Society's reference library contains more than 2,000 volumes, and there are more than 1,300 files with information on families, historic buildings, events and sites, plus a map and photograph collection. This is the best place to begin.

> **FIND IT: 130 Caroline Street, Orange, Virginia 229130.**
> Follow I-64 West to exit 136 onto US-15N, and turn right. Go about 12 miles to a traffic circle. Enter the circle and go all the way around to stay on US-15N/Caroline Street. In about 9 miles stay straight. The Historical Society is ahead on the left, with rows of small boxwoods in the front. There is ample parking in the front as well. The library is open from 1-5 PM.
> **(540) 672.5366   orangecovahist.org**

ORIGINAL DOCUMENTS

Orange County Clerk of the Circuit Court has most court records from 1734.

> **FIND IT: 110 North Madison Street, Orange, VA 229130.**
> From the Historical Society drive back down Caroline Street just a short way. Turn left onto South Madison Rd/US-15. When you cross Main Street the Courthouse will be on your left. Just on down the hill is the entrance to the parking lot. Enter the Courthouse through security. Take the elevator up to the 3rd floor

and follow the signs to the Clerk's office. Ask for a guide
sheet to books in the genealogy room. A copy card is needed
for the copier. **(540) 672.3150**

GOOD TO KNOW

Orange Co Visitor Center 122 E Main Street, Orange, VA 22960
Located in the Historic Orange Train Station find brochures, maps
and free information about Orange County Virginia
(877) 222.8072   visitorangevirginia.com

The James Madison Museum houses exhibits on James and Dolly
Madison, featuring one of the nation's most outstanding collections
of Madisonia. On display are a number of James' and Dolly's personal
items, papers, and furnishings. The Museum is across the street from
the Historical Society. **thejamesmadisonmuseum.org**

Montpelier is the lifelong home of James Madison, Father of the
Constitution, architect of the Bill of Rights, and President of the
United States. **montpelier.org**

PAGE COUNTY

Page County was formed in 1831 from Shenandoah and Rockingham counties. It was named for John Page, Governor of Virginia from 1802 to 1805. The county seat is Luray.

 **WHERE TO START**

FAMILY RESEARCH

The Page County Public Library is the best place to begin. The Library owns a large Genealogical and Historical section. This collection includes a pamphlet collection of material dealing with Page County and the collection of the *Page News & Courier* microfilmed newspaper from 1869 through present. There is a printed index to family folders. Don't miss the nice little park across the street.

> **FIND IT: 100 Zerkel Street, Luray, VA 22835** Take I-64 W and exit #136 onto US-15N. Turn right and go about 12 miles. In the traffic circle take the 2nd exit onto US-33W/North Main Street. Go about 33 miles and merge right onto US-33Bus toward Front Royal. Go about 17 miles and turn right onto Lee Hwy/US-211. In about 6 miles bear right onto West Main Street/US-211Bus. In about 1 mile turn right onto Firehouse Lane which turns into Zerkle Street. The Library is ahead on the corner of Zerkle and Campbell.
> **(540) 743.6867   www.mrlib/pagecountylibrary**

ORIGINAL DOCUMENTS

Page County Clerk of the Circuit Court: All the records for Page County are in the Record Room. The Will Books are in a separate room and Chancery records are on microfilm. Ask for permission to use a camera.

FIND IT: 116 South Court Street, Luray, VA 22835 From the Library parking lot head back toward the silos and turn left onto Campbell Street. Stay on Campbell/ Broad Street to West Main Street and turn left. Go down Main, cross the creek and the take the 4th left onto Court Street. The Courthouse is up the hill. Take the first right onto West Page Street to enter the parking lot. Enter through the front. The Clerk's Office is on the main level to the left of the front door. **(540) 743.4064**

GOOD TO KNOW

The Luray-Page County Chamber of Commerce, 18 Campbell St., Luray, VA 22835 is located in the renovated train station in downtown Luray. The chamber office also serves as the Visitor Center, where staff and dedicated volunteers greet tourists and answer their questions about Luray & Page County. **(540) 743.3915   luraypage.com**

Warehouse Art Gallery, 15 Campbell Street, Luray, VA 22835 has world-class art in a 7000 sq. ft., casual gallery with outstanding local and regional artists; extensive sculpture gallery. **(540) 843.0200   warehouseartcenter.net**

Luray Caverns is eastern America's largest natural Landmark. There are cathedral-size rooms with ceilings 10 stores high filled with ancient stone formations. Experience the haunting sounds of the world's largest musical instrument, The Great Stalacpipe Organ. 970 US Hwy 211 West, Luray, VA 22835. **(540) 743.6551 x250   luraycaverns.com**

PATRICK COUNTY

Patrick County was formed in 1791, from Patrick Henry County. The older part of the county became just Henry County. Patrick County was named for Patrick Henry. The county seat is Stuart.

 **WHERE TO START**

FAMILY RESEARCH

Patrick County Historical Society and Museum: The genealogy section contains family histories compiled by a number of noted genealogists, and there are birth, death, and marriage records that have been extracted from the courthouse records including nearby counties.

> **FIND IT: 116 West Blue Ridge Street, Stuart, VA 24171**
> From Richmond find your way to VA-288S to US-360W toward Amelia County and then down to South Boston via US-360/15. Continue on to and around Danville on US-58/Danville Expressway towards Martinsville. In about 15 miles, take the US-58 by-pass around Martinsville. In about 10 miles take the US-58 W exit towards Stuart which will merge onto US-58Bus/Philpott Hwy. US-58 will become Jeb Stuart Hwy in about 9 miles. In 14 miles turn left onto E Blue Ridge Street. It becomes W Blue Ridge at Main Street and the Courthouse. Continue on about .5 miles to the Historical Society up on the right. It shares the space with the Patrick County Library. Watch for signs inside the front door. **(276) 694.2840 patcovhistory.org**

ORIGINAL DOCUMENTS

Patrick County Clerk of the Circuit Court has original records available for research. There is an index to marriages but no original bonds. No cameras are allowed.

FIND IT: 101 Blue Ridge Street, Stuart, VA 24171-0148
Follow the directions to the Historical Society. The Courthouse
is in the center of town. Just go back the way you came and park
on the street. The Entrance to the Clerk's Office is around to the
right from the front of the building.

GOOD TO KNOW

Bob White Covered Bridge is a rare 80-foot queen post
construction over the Smith River that was built in 1921.
The 48-foot oak-constructed **Jack's Creek Covered Bridge** was
built in 1914 by Charles Vaughan and designed by Walter Weaver
of Woolwine. **(276) 694-8367   visitpatrickcounty.org**

Fairy Stone State Park, 967 Fairystone Lake Dr., Stuart, VA, 24171,
is the home of the legendary fairy stones, this park is well known for its
168-acre lake adjoining Philpott Reservoir. The park is just minutes from
the Blue Ridge Parkway. **(276) 930.2424**

**The Wood Brothers Racing Museum, 21 Performance Drive, Stuart,
VA 24171,** is located just 30 minutes from Martinsville Speedway.
Wood Brothers Racing is one of the oldest continuously operating teams
in NASCAR. **(276) 694.2121   woodbrothersracing.com**

Mabry Mill 266 Mill Rd, mi 176, Meadows of Dan, VA 24120,
is an iconic structure along the Blue Ridge Parkway. The grist mill is
still in operation. **mabrymillrestaurant.com**

PITTSYLVANIA COUNTY

The county was formed in 1767 from Halifax County. It was named for William Pitt, 1st Earl of Chatham. The county seat is Chatham.

 WHERE TO START

FAMILY RESEARCH

History and Research Center of the Pittsylvania County Public Library in Chatham has a significant collection of materials related to the history of the county and its people."

> **FIND IT: 340 Whitehead Street, Chatham, VA 24531** Make your way to VA-288 South and exit US-360 W/Hull Street toward Amelia. In about 88 miles turn right onto VA-360 W/Bethel Road. In about 7 miles turn right onto US-501 N. In about 7 miles turn left onto Rte 642. In about 3 miles turn right onto VA-57 W/Halifax Road. In 22 miles turn right onto S Main Street. Take the first left onto Depot Street. Watch for the Railroad underpass and turn left just before it onto Whitehead Street. The Historical Society and Library is ahead on the right. **(434) 432.8931 hc.pcplib.org**

Piedmont Genealogical Society has more than 5,000 books and covers the Virginia counties of Franklin, Henry, Pittsylvania and Halifax and the North Carolina counties of Person, Rockingham, and Caswell.

> **FIND IT: 511 Patton Street, Danville, VA 24541** From the Courthouse in Chatham follow South Main Street/US-29 for about 16 miles and merge onto US-360/US-58 Bus. In about 3 miles turn left onto VA-293 S. Cross the Dan River and turn left onto Memorial Drive. Take the first right onto Patton Street. As you pass the Danville Courthouse and start up the hill, watch for

the Library ahead on the left at the corner of Court and Patton.
Continue on Patton to the parking lot behind the building.
(434) 799.5195

ORIGINAL DOCUMENTS

Pittsylvania County Clerk of the Circuit Court has most
original records from 1767.

> **FIND IT: One North Main Street, Chatham, VA** From the
> Historical Society go back left on Collie Street, right on Depot
> Street and left on Main Street. The Courthouse is ahead on the
> right. The Clerk's Office is at ground level to the right of the
> large stairway. Park on the street.

GOOD TO KNOW

Crossing at the Dan, a renovated railroad yard; includes a Science
Center, a Community Market, and walking trails along the **Dan River.**
(434) 793.4636   danville-va.gov

Simpson Funeral Museum, 16 S. Main St in Chatham. The museum
features murals covering a history of funerary services dating back
thousands of years and replicas of caskets for famous people.

Callands Clerk's Office, Courthouse and Gaol, served as the County's
first county seat from 1767-1777. Guides to area walking and driving
tours available at this web site. **(434) 432.1650   victorianvilla.com**

Danville Science Center. **(434) 791.5160   dsc.smv.org**

1813 Clerk's Office houses a small museum behind Chatham Town Hall
and at the edge of Francis Hallam Hurt Park. The park is open daily and
the museum by appointment. **pittsylvaniahistoricalsociety.org**

POWHATAN COUNTY

Powhatan County was formed in 1777 from the eastern end of Cumberland County. The county was named in honor of Chief Powhatan, the father of Pocahontas. The county seat is Powhatan.

 WHERE TO START

FAMILY RESEARCH

The Goochland County Historical Society: Goochland is the parent county of Powhatan. This library contains an extensive family file collection and volunteers who are helpful to the novice researcher.

> **FIND IT: 2875 River Road West, Goochland, VA 23063**
> See Goochland County for directions.

ORIGINAL DOCUMENTS

Powhatan County Clerk of the Circuit Court has complete original records from 1777.

> **FIND IT: 3880 Old Buckingham Rd, Powhatan, VA 23139**
> From Goochland make your way back east on VA-6 to VA-288 S to merge onto Midlothian Turnpike/US-60 W. In about 13 miles turn left onto VA-300 S. This road will dead-end into Tilman Road. Turn left and take the next slight right onto VA-1004. Go one block and turn right onto VA-13 W/ Old Buckingham Road. The Courthouse is ahead on the right. Park on the street and follow the sidewalk around to the right. The Clerk's Office is well marked.
> **(804) 598.5660**

GOOD TO KNOW

Huguenot Society of the Founders of Manakin, 981 Huguenot Trail, Midlothian, VA 23113 This small library is housed in the headquarters of the Manakin Huguenot Society, and is staffed by a certified librarian. The collection of 700+ volumes focuses on Virginia genealogy and history and Huguenot history. A catalog is available on the website.
(804) 794.5702   huguenot-manakin.org

Powhatan County Library, 2270 Mann Road Powhatan, VA 23139
The library has a small local history section which include family files and other resources. It is about 1 mile from the Courthouse.
(804) 598.5670

Fighting Creek Park: This 220 acre park is home to the Powhatan Public Library, the National Guard Armory, the YMCA, numerous athletic fields, a large playground, walking trails, and picnic shelters. Powhatan County Courthouse: On the National Register of Historic Places, it was designed by noted New York architect Alexander Jackson Davis and completed in 1849 in the Greek revival style of architecture.

Other points of interest include the "Old Jail" which houses the Powhatan Historical Society, a lovely garden depicting area flowers, plants, and vegetables, a historic tavern, and several other historic buildings.

During the American Civil war, after the fall of Richmond, a large Confederate wagon supply train, led by General Lee's oldest son, Custis, passed through here. The much needed supplies were headed to General Lee in Amelia, but never got there. The wagons were captured shortly after crossing the Appomattox River into Amelia.

PRINCE EDWARD COUNTY

Prince Edward County was formed in 1754 from Amelia County. It was named for Prince Edward, second son of Frederick, Prince of Wales and younger brother of King George III of the United Kingdom. The county seat is Farmville.

WHERE TO START

FAMILY RESEARCH

There is no repository for family files in Prince Edward County. The Prince Edward Farmville Library does have some resource materials. The researcher would do well to visit the Amelia Historical Society (See Amelia County) and the South Central Genealogical Society in Charlotte Court House. (See Charlotte County). Both sites are nearby.

ORIGINAL DOCUMENTS

Prince Edward County Clerk of the Circuit Court has most court documents from 1754. An index to marriages is available in the record room but the marriage bonds are on microfilm at the Library of Virginia. Ask about the card file for deaths and burials.

> **FIND IT: 111 N South St # 3, Farmville, VA 23901** Farmville is about an hour's drive from Richmond. Make your west and south to VA-288 S. Exit onto US-60W toward Powhatan. In about 36 miles turn left onto VA-45 S toward Farmville. Careful! This turn is easy to miss. In about 15 miles turn left onto E 3rd Street and take the first right onto South Street. There is ample parking along South Street. Enter the Courthouse through the rear entrance and take the elevator to the second floor street level. Turn left. The Clerk's Office is down the hall on the right. **(434) 392.5145**

GOOD TO KNOW

The **Moton Museum, 900 Griffin Blvd, Farmville, VA 23903** is the site of the once all Black High School where students walked out during the 1950's on a two week strike opposing the deplorable conditions for learning. Discover how the Civil Rights Movement in this country began right here in Prince Edward County at this former High School. It is affiliated with Longwood University.

High Bridge Trail Park, 6888 Green Bay Rd, Green Bay, VA High Bridge Trail State Park, a rails to trails linear state park opened April 2012 as one of the newest Virginia's State Parks. The park's centerpiece is the majestic High Bridge, which is more than 2,400 feet long and 125 feet above the Appomattox River.

Worsham Clerks office is the site of the original Prince Edward County Court House in the village of Worsham, VA. Find it on Route 15 south toward Keysville.

The Virginia's Retreat region of South Central Virginia offers the nation's first Civil War History Trail, the Lee's Retreat driving tour and the Wilson-Kautz Raid Civil War driving tours and is home to the Civil Rights in Education Heritage Trail. **varetreat.com**

Hampden-Sydney College 1 College Road Farmville, VA 23901 is a private, liberal arts college for men.

PRINCE GEORGE COUNTY

Prince George County was formed in 1703 from Charles City County. It was named for Prince George of Denmark, husband of Anne, Queen of Great Britain. The county seat is Prince George.

 WHERE TO START

FAMILY RESEARCH

The Ann K. & Preston H. Leake Local History & Genealogy Room: Located on the 2nd floor of the Appomattox Regional Library, in Hopewell, VA, the Room has extensive family files and records about Charles City County, Prince George County, and Dinwiddie County. This is the best place to begin.

> **FIND IT: 209 E Cawson St, Hopewell, VA 23860** Exit #61A from I-95 South onto VA-10 E/ W Hundred Road. In about 8 miles turn left onto N Main Street and take the 1st right onto E Cawson Street. The Library is ahead on the left. There is on street parking and two large lots adjacent to the Library. **(804) 458.6329x2008   arls.org**

ORIGINAL DOCUMENTS

Prince George County Clerk of the Circuit Court had most of its early records destroyed during the American Civil War. Complete records exist from 1843 to the present.

> **FIND IT: 6601 Courts Drive, Prince George, VA 23875** From the Library in Hopewell, go back to N Main Street and turn left. Take the 1st left onto VA-10 E. In about 3 miles turn right onto VA-306/ VA-156 bypass. In about 6 miles turn right onto Laurel Spring Road and take the first left onto Courts Drive. Enter through security. **(804) 733.2623**

GOOD TO KNOW

The **Prince George County Library, 6605 Courts Drive, Prince George, VA 23875** was constructed to reflect the values and rural influences of Prince George County. The Library features an art gallery and is adjacent to the County Courthouse and Scott Park. **(804) 458.6329x3700**

Pamplin Historical Park and The National Museum of the Civil War Soldier is recognized as one of America's premier historical attractions and as the most innovative Civil War history park in the country. **pamplinpark.org**

Poplar Grove National Cemetery, 8005 Vaughan Road, Dinwiddie, VA 23841: "Where Valor Proudly Sleeps". Places like Poplar Grove National Cemetery reflect the tragedy of the American Civil War. It is closed for burials but the grounds are open every day.

Appomattox Plantation, 1001 Pecan Avenue, Hopewell, 23860: A land patent granted to Captain Francis Eppes at City Point in 1635. The plantation house was built in 1763. It served as headquarters for General Grant circa 1864-65. Annexed by the City of Hopewell in 1923, it is now owned and operated by the National Park Service as a part of the Petersburg National Battlefield.

Jordan's Point and the Bland Family Cemetery at the site of the family home on Jordan's Point. Believed to be the burial site of Richard Bland along with thirty-eight other family members. Owned and maintained by the Prince George Regional Heritage Center.

PRINCE WILLIAM COUNTY

Prince William County was formed in 1731 from the western section of
Stafford County and a part of King George County. It was named for
Prince William, Duke of Cumberland, and third son of King George II.
The county seat is Manassas.

WHERE TO START

FAMILY RESEARCH

Bull Run Regional Library houses the Ruth E. Lloyd Information Center
(RELIC), a special collection devoted to genealogy and local history with
a focus on Virginia and Prince William County. This is the best place to
begin. The staff are trained to help trace family history and to research
persons, places and events associated with local history.

> **FIND IT: 8051 Ashton Ave.,** Manassas, **VA 20109-2892**. From
> Richmond follow I-95 N and exit 152B to merge on US-234
> W/Prince William Parkway. In about 20 miles turn right onto
> Sudley Manor Drive. In about 1 ½ miles turn left onto Ashton
> Avenue. At the first traffic light turn right into the parking lot.
> The Library entrance faces away from Ashton Ave.
> **(703) 792.4540   pwcgov.org/library/relic**

ORIGINAL DOCUMENTS

Prince William County Clerk of the Circuit Court has records
from 1863. Many Deed and Will books prior to 1861 are missing.

> **FIND IT: 9311 Lee Ave., Manassas, VA 20109.** From the
> Library parking lot turn left at the traffic light to go back south
> on Ashton Ave. Continue on through the intersection at Sudley
> Manor Drive to the next traffic light at Crestwood Drive and turn
> left. Follow Crestwood until it ends at Sudley Road and turn right.
> In about 2 miles bear right onto Grant Ave. In less than 1 mile
> turn right onto Lee Ave. The new Courthouse is ahead on the left.
> All parking adjacent to the building is reserved. Drive through

this lot to a free public lot across a side street. Enter the building through security and walk back to elevators on the right. The Public Service Center is on the 3rd floor and down Hallway #1.

GOOD TO KNOW

Manassas Visitor Center, 9431 West Street, Manassas, VA offers brochures, maps, and a friendly knowledgeable staff. It is located in the 1914 Manassas Train Depot. **visitmanassas.org/visitorscenter**

Visitor Center, 200 Mill Street, Occoquan, VA 22125. Located in the heart of historic Occoquan, the Visitor Center provides tourist information and is within walking distance of specialty shops, unique restaurants and the riverfront. Closed on Monday and Tuesday. **(703) 491.4057   discoverpwm.com**

Rippon Lodge, 15520 Blackburn Rd, Woodbridge VA 2219. Built circa 1747 Rippon Lodge is one of the oldest known homes in Prince William County. Extensive restoration work began at Rippon Lodge in 2000 and was completed in 2007 when the site opened for public tours. **(703) 499.9812**

Manassas Battlefield National Park, Henry Hill Visitor Center, 6511 Sudley Road, Manassas, VA 20109
On July 21, 1861, two armies clashed for the first time on the fields overlooking Bull Run. Heavy fighting swept away any notion of a quick war. In August 1862, Union and Confederate armies met for a second time on the plains of Manassas. The Confederates won a solid victory bringing them to the height of their power. **nps.gov/mana**

PULASKI COUNTY

Pulaski County was formed in 1839 from parts of Montgomery and Wythe counties. It was named for a Polish Count, Casimir Pulaski, who fought during the American Revolution as part of George Washington's army. The county seat is Pulaski.

 WHERE TO START

FAMILY RESEARCH

The Wilderness Road Regional Museum in Dublin, VA is the best place to begin.

> **FIND IT: 5240 Wilderness Road, Dublin, Virginia 24084**
> From Richmond make your way to I-64 West and I-81 South. Exit #98 ramp and turn left onto VA-100N toward Dublin. In about 1 mile turn left again onto State Road 611. The museum is about ½ mile ahead on the left at the corner of Wilderness Road and Townes Ferry Road, a big white house with big blue shutters.
> **(540) 674.4835** **wildernessroadregionalmuseum.com**

ORIGINAL DOCUMENTS

Pulaski County Clerk of the Circuit Court has most records from 1839.

> **FIND IT: 45 3rd St NW, Pulaski, VA 24301** From the museum go back on State Road 611 across I-81 and continue into the town of Pulaski. This road will dead-end at East Main Street. Turn right and continue across US-11. The Courthouse is ahead on the left. Note: 3rd Street is one-way. Park on the street. To reach the Clerk's Office go in through this new entrance and ask for the Record Room. This is an impressive rough cut stone building and should be seen from the front to really appreciate the arches and the clock tower. **(540) 980.7825**

GOOD TO KNOW

The Pulaski County Library, 60 Third St. NW, Pulaski, VA 24301
has a small family history room with family files, and cemetery records.
Continue on Third Street past the Courthouse. The Library is ahead on
the right. **(540) 980.7770**

Pulaski County Courthouse To see and learn more about the history
of Pulaski County, visit the Historic 1896 Stone Courthouse, restored
following a devastating fire in 1992. The courthouse has exhibits
showcasing the county's history including artifacts from pre-historic
times and its settlement. Use the Main Street entrance.

Pulaski Theatre 14 W Main Street, Pulaski, VA 24301 opened as
a vaudeville house in 1911. It has been restored and is now open for
business. Find them on social media.

Historic Howe House in **Claytor State Park 6620 Bolen Drive,
Dublin,VA 24084** has interactive exhibits describing the ecology of the
lake and the surrounding areas. **claytor-lake.net**

The New River cuts through beautiful VA mountain scenery and features
several major Class II-III rapids for white water rafting. The New River
is recognized as one of two American Heritage rivers in Virginia.

Calfee Ball Park is home to the Pulaski Mariners, a farm team for
the Seattle Mariners. The original covered grandstand still stands.
pulaskitown.org/calfee_park

Randolph Park is a six million dollar state-of-the-art outdoor
recreational facility that sits on 87 acres in Pulaski County.
randolphpark.org

RAPPAHANOCK COUNTY

Rappahannock County was formed in 1833 from Culpeper County. Rappahannock County was named for the river that separates it from Fauquier County. The county seat is Washington.

 **WHERE TO START**

FAMILY RESEARCH

The Rappahannock Historical Society: Library holdings include family files, birth, death, marriage, and will records for Rappahannock and surrounding counties. The museum contains artifacts of the county, some of which are prehistoric. This is the best place to begin.

> **FIND IT: 328 Gay Street, Washington, VA 22747** Travel north on I-95 to exit #133 and merge onto US-17 N toward Warrenton. In about 27 miles US-17 becomes Opal Road. Stay straight for about 5 more miles. Turn left onto Springs Road. In about 3 miles it becomes VA-621. Continue on about 4 more miles and turn left onto US-211 W/ Lee Highway. In 12 miles turn right onto US-211Bus E/Warren Ave. In less than ½ mile take the second left onto Gay Street. Watch for the Historical Society ahead on the left. Park on the street.
> **(540) 675.1163   rappahannockhistsoc.org**

ORIGINAL DOCUMENTS

Rappahannock County Clerk of the Circuit Court has most all of the court records from its founding in 1833.

> **FIND IT: 238 Gay Street, Washington, VA 22747** From the Historical Society continue on down Gay Street to the Courthouse Complex. Enter the Clerk's Office located to the right as you face the Courthouse. Park on the street.
> **(540) 675.5350**

GOOD TO KNOW

The town of Washington was established by the Virginia General Assembly in 1796, chosen as the County seat in 1833, and incorporated in 1894. Other historical villages in the County are Amissville, Chester Gap, Flint Hill, and Sperryville.

The Scrabble School, a Rosenwald School built in 1921 houses the Rappahannock African-American Heritage Center, which features an exhibit that tells the story of the school, the community it once served, and its place in local, state, and national history.
(540) 222.1457 scrabbleschool.org

The Inn at Little Washington opened in 1978 and over the last quarter century has evolved from a simple country inn to an international culinary shrine. The Inn's twenty-four bedrooms and suites are sumptuous hideaways created by Joyce Evans, a London stage and set designer, **theinnatlittlewashington.com**

visitrappahannockva.com for a complete listing of things occurring in Rappahannock.

RICHMOND COUNTY

Richmond County was formed in 1692 from the original Rappahannock County. It has been accepted that the county was named for the First Duke of Richmond, cousin to King William and Queen Mary. The county seat is Warsaw.

WHERE TO START

FAMILY RESEARCH

The Westmoreland County Museum and Visitor Center is the best place to begin. They do have family files and other resources available for research. It is about a 15 minute drive to Warsaw from here.

> **FIND IT: 43 Court Square, Montross, Virginia 22520**
> From Richmond take I-64 East to exit 192 and merge onto US-360 E. Go about 43 miles and turn right onto US-360 E/Queen Street. Go about 7 miles and turn left onto Main Street. In less than a mile turn left onto VA-3. In about 12 miles bear right onto Court Square. The Museum is ahead on the right.
> **(804) 493.8440   inwestmoreland.com**

ORIGINAL DOCUMENTS

Richmond County Clerk of the Circuit Court has probate and land records from 1692.

> **FIND IT: 101 Court Circle Warsaw, VA 22572-0956** The Courthouse in Warsaw is a 15 minute drive from the Historical Society in Montross. Make your way back onto VA-3 E. In about 12 miles turn right onto Main Street. In about .8 mile go straight through the green light across US-360 and bear left onto Court Circle. This is an odd intersection! The Clerk's office is a long brick building on the left. Watch for the sign. Park on the street.
> **(804) 333.3781**

GOOD TO KNOW

The Library of **Rappahannock Community College, Warsaw Campus, 52 Campus Drive,** is also the home of the **Richmond County Public Library.** This is one of the first joint ventures of its kind in Virginia. The local history collection has books in print about Richmond County and the Northern Neck. The Library also has on Microfilm most issues from 1879 of *The Northern Neck News.*
(804) 333.6710   rcplva.org

The Richmond County Museum, 5874 Richmond Road, Warsaw, VA 22572 is located in the Old Jail on the Courthouse Green.
(804) 333.3607   co.richmond.va.us/visitors

Menokin, 4037 Menokin Rd., Warsaw, VA 22572 was the home of Declaration of Independence signer Francis Lightfoot Lee circa 1769. The Visitors center depicting architectural conservation using glass walls and existing portions of the original house is underway. Hike trails to Cat Point Creek through the 325-acre **Rappahannock River Valley National Wildlife Refuge. 804.333.1776   menokin.org**

Naylor's Beach, 4011 Naylor's Beach Road, Warsaw, VA 22572 is a campground and boating site on the Rappahannock River. The USA Mid-Atlantic Triathlon was held here in June of 2015.

Mount Airy Plantation, Warsaw, VA is the ancestral home of the Tayloe family. It is one of the few stone houses built in the 1700s in Virginia. It is not open to the public but is available for events.
mountairyplantation.com

co.richmond.va.us/community provides an excellent overview to tourism opportunities in Richmond County.

ROANOKE COUNTY

The county was formed in 1838 from the southern part of Botetourt County. Land from Montgomery County was added in 1845. Roanoke is a Native American term for money. The county seat is Salem.

 **WHERE TO START**

FAMILY RESEARCH

Roanoke Public Library: The Virginia Room in the Main Library is the best place to begin. The Library's collection of historical and genealogical research includes items relating to the entire state and its people. Ask for the collection guide brochure.

> **FIND IT: 706 S Jefferson Street, Roanoke, VA 24016**
> From I-81 S exit #143 on the left onto I-581 S/US-220 toward Airport/Roanoke. In about 6 miles exit # 5 toward Downtown and merge onto Williamson Rd NE and next right onto Franklin Road SE, then next left onto S Jefferson Street. The building is ahead on the left. There is a parking garage directly across the street. **(540) 342.5770   roanokeva.gov/libraries**

ORIGINAL DOCUMENTS

Roanoke County Clerk of the Circuit Court has most documents from 1838 available for research. This record room is large and inviting and the deputy clerks are very willing to help.

> **FIND IT: 305 E. Main Street, Salem, VA 24153-1126**   From the Library go back along S Jefferson Street and turn right onto Franklin Rd SE. Take the next left onto Williamson Rd SE. In about 1 mile turn left onto Orange Ave/Salem Turn-Pike. In about 2 miles bear slight right onto Melrose Ave NW which becomes E Main Street. The Courthouse is ahead on the right. It is a handsome, contemporary beige brick building. There is paid

parking across the street or free parking behind the convenience store at the corner of Clay and Main Streets just before you reach the Courthouse. Enter between the columns through security. **(540) 387.6205**

GOOD TO KNOW

Salem Museum and Historical Society, **801 East Main Street, Salem, VA 24153** The Salem Museum exhibit galleries are self-guided and handicapped accessible. **(540) 389.6760** **salemmuseum.org**

Mill Mountain Zoo Mill Mountain Park, Roanoke, VA 24014 is an AZA accredited five-acre zoo, with more than 161 mammals, birds and reptiles. **(540) 343.3241** **mmzoo.org**

Taubman Art Museum, 110 Salem Ave SW, Roanoke, VA 24011 **(540) 342.5760** **taubmanmuseum.org**

Dixie Caverns 5753 West Main Street, Salem, VA 24153 Guided tours through these caverns that highlight a large number of still-growing stalagmites and stalactites. **(540) 380.2085**

Salem Red Sox 1004 Texas Street, Salem, VA 24153 The Salem Red Sox are a Minor League Baseball team in Salem, Virginia, an independent city adjacent to Roanoke, Virginia. It is a Class High-A team in the Carolina League and a farm team of the Boston Red Sox. **(540) 389.3333**

Carvins Cove Natural Reserve 9644 Reservoir Road, Roanoke, VA 24019 The Reserve is the second largest city park in the United States, at 12,700 acres. It is located in Botetourt County, Virginia and Roanoke County, Virginia. Recreational activities, such as mountain biking, hiking, and equestrian activities, are allowed around the reservoir. **(540) 563.9170**

ROCKBRIDGE COUNTY

Rockbridge County was established in 1778 from Augusta County and Botetourt County. It was named for Natural Bridge, a naturally formed bridge in the south of the county. The county seat is Lexington.

 **WHERE TO START**

FAMILY RESEARCH

Campbell House is the home of the **Rockbridge Historical Society.** The Society's collection of historic documents for genealogy is maintained in the archives of **Washington and Lee University James Leyburn library**. This catalogued collection is free and open to the public.

> **FIND IT: 101 E. Washington St. Lexington, VA 24450-1409.** From I-81 south exit #195 onto US-11 toward Lexington. In about 5 miles turn slight right onto N Main Street which will become N Jefferson. In about 1 mile turn left onto W Nelson Street. Stay on Nelson across N Main Street and take the next left onto S Randolph Street. The Courthouse is here on the corner. There is free parking just down Randolph Street on the right, behind the Courthouse. Walk on down Randolph one block to the Historical Society. The Lexington Visitors Center is across the street with parking if you choose to drive.
> **(540) 464.1058 rockhist.org**

> **FIND IT: James Leyburn Library, 204 W Washington Street, Lexington, VA 24450.** From the Historical Society continue on West Washington Street to the University. Turn left onto Lee Avenue and right onto Nelson Street. There is a parking garage along this street on the right. The Library is in the center of campus just a brief walk from the garage. Please call Security for parking advice if needed. **(540) 458.8400.**
> **(540) 458.8643 library.wlu.edu**

ORIGINAL DOCUMENTS

Rockbridge County Clerk of the Circuit Court has land, probate, civil and marriage records from 1778.

> **FIND IT: 20 South Randolph Street, Lexington, VA, 24450.** From the Historical Society walk back up S Randolph street to enter the Courthouse building through security. Ask for the Record Room. **(540) 463-2232**

GOOD TO KNOW

Natural Bridge, 15 Appledore Ln, Natural Bridge, VA 24578 is a geological formation in which Cedar Creek has carved out a gorge forming a natural arch 215 ft high with a span of 90 ft.

Cyrus McCormick Farm,128 McCormick Farm Cir, Raphine, VA 24472 Cyrus McCormick invented the reaper near Steele's Tavern at the northern end of the county. **(540) 377.2255**

Stonewall Jackson House, 8 E Washington Street, Lexington, VA 24450 (540) 463.2552 visitstonewall.com

Wade's Mill 55 Kennedy-Wades Mill, Raphine, VA 24472 is a working water-powered mill, circa 1750, on the National Register of Historic Places. **(800) 290.1400**

Brownsburg Museum, 2716 Brownsburg Turnpike, Brownsburg, VA 24415 This amazing community-run museum is in the heart of the picturesque Village of Brownsburg. **(540) 348.1600**

rootsweb.ancestry.com/varags/references has a summary of local reference sites for Rockbridge County compiled by the Rockbridge Area Genealogical Society (RAGS).

ROCKINGHAM COUNTY

Rockingham County was formed in 1778 from Augusta and Botetourt Counties. It is named for Charles Watson-Wentworth, the second Marquis of Rockingham. The county seat is Harrisonburg.

 **WHERE TO START**

FAMILY RESEARCH

Massanutten Regional Library Genealogy & Local History Room contains more than 5,000 items documenting the families and history of Rockingham County and the Shenandoah Valley.

> **FIND IT: 174 S Main St, Harrisonburg, VA 22801** Follow I-64 W and exit #87 toward Winchester, VA to merge onto I-81 N. In about 24 miles exit #245 and turn right onto VA-253/Port Republic Road. In about ½ mile turn right onto Lee Highway/ S Main Street. This road goes through James Madison University campus. It divides just past MLK Jr Way. S Main Street is one-way going into town (N) and Lee Street is one-way (S) out of town. The Library is at the corner of S Main and Bruce Streets. As you pass Asbury Methodist Church take the next right onto Bruce Street for Library Parking. **(540) 434.4475   mrlib.org**

ORIGINAL DOCUMENTS

Rockingham County Clerk of the Circuit Court has records from 1778 but some of the records were burned. The County web site offers an overview to the records that exist.

> **FIND IT:** 80 Court Square, Harrisonburg, VA 22801 From the Library continue along S Main Street about .2 of a mile. Turn left onto Court Square at the Harrisonburg City Public School Building. Follow Court Square all the way around. Park and enter through security under the Clock Tower. Ask for the Deed Room. **(540) 564.3126**

GOOD TO KNOW

The Heritage Museum of the Harrisonburg-Rockingham Historical Society 382 High Street, Dayton, VA 22821, is another excellent place for research. The Museum is about 10 minutes from the Library and Courthouse. It serves as the Welcome Center to Historic Dayton as well. **(540) 879.2616   heritagecenter.com**

The Hardesty-Higgins House Visitor Center is across Bruce Street from the Library.   **visitharrisonburgva.com**

Endless Caverns, 1800 Endless Caverns Rd, New Market, VA 22844
Located at the foot of the Massanutten Mountain range, Endless Caverns has been thrilling visitors with a spectacular display of formations presented in their natural coloring since 1920.
(540) 896.2283   endlesscaverns.com

Grand Caverns, 5 Grand Caverns Drive, Grottoes, VA 24441
Cathedral Hall is 280 feet long and more than 70 feet high.
(540) 249.5705   grandcaverns.com

Virginia Quilt Museum, 301 S Main Street, Harrisonburg, VA 22801
The Museum features a permanent collection of nearly 300 quilts, a Civil War Gallery, antique and toy sewing machines, and rotating exhibits from across the United States.   **(540) 433.3818**

RUSSELL COUNTY

Russell was formed in 1786 from Washington County. The county was named for Culpeper County native Colonel William Russell. The county seat is Lebanon.

 **WHERE TO START**

FAMILY RESEARCH

Russell County Library: Go first to the Library. In the local history room you will find family books and files, indexes to transcribed records, and much more to get you started.

> **FIND IT: 248 W. Main Street, Lebanon, VA, 24266.**
> From I-81 south, take exit #17 and turn right onto VA-75N. In .5 mile turn left onto US-58, go three (3) blocks, and turn right onto Russell Ave. In about 1 mile merge right onto US-19N. In about 18 miles, take Exit 1 onto US-19 Bus/West Main Street toward Lebanon and turn left. The Library is about a mile ahead on the left. It is located just a few blocks west of the Courthouse.
> **(276) 889.8044   russell.lib.va.us**

ORIGINAL DOCUMENTS

Russell County Clerk of the Circuit Court has all of the Deed and Will Books available. Marriage book 1 is not available, it was lost. Existing marriage records begin in 1849. Ask a clerk about copies of wills.

> **FIND IT: 53 E. Main Street, Lebanon, VA 24266**
> Follow directions to the Library. Cross Church Street where West Main becomes East Main. The Clerk's Office is in the Courthouse. Enter the front doors of the Courthouse and turn left into the Clerk's Office. **(276) 889.8023**

GOOD TO KNOW

The Dante Coal Mining and Railroad Museum, 30 Straight Hollow Road, Dante, VA 24237. The Coal Miner's Memorial is nearby.

Hungarian Cemetery located between the towns of Hamlin and Sun just off Rte 63 in Russell County. The Russell County Public Library has a transcribed list of the grave stones from this cemetery that have been translated into English.

The Clinch River has been ranked the #1 river in the country by the Nature Conservancy for environmental diversity and significance and is the top river in the world for freshwater mussels.

The Town of Dante annually hosts a celebration of their town, usually in August, see www.danteliveson.org. It was once a mining town and efforts are being made to preserve that history and heritage.

Elk Garden Church, founded in 1788, is most likely the second oldest church in Russell County. It is near an original fort on the Clinch River Frontier.

Saint Paul, Virginia Town Hall, 16531 Russell Street, St. Paul, VA 24283 is a town on US-58 Alt in the corner of Wise and Russell Counties. "Where the coalfields meet the bluegrass", St. Paul is a place of natural beauty on the Clinch River. The Historic District includes the 1887 Ennis House, and the 1901 St. Paul Hotel. Much of the town of St. Paul is in Wise County.

The St. Paul Loop - Virginia Birding and Wildlife Trail: The Loop offers six excellent sites in proximity to the Town of Saint Paul.

SCOTT COUNTY

Scott County was formed in 1814 from parts of Washington, Lee, and Russell Counties. It was named for Virginia born General Winfield Scott. The county seat is Gate City.

 WHERE TO START

FAMILY RESEARCH

The Scott County Public Library has a small research room of family histories, maps, and other aids to help the researcher get started.

> **FIND IT: 297 West Jackson Street, Gate City, VA 24251**
> Follow I-81 South all the way to Bristol and cross into Tennessee. Exit #74 B toward Kingsport and merge onto US-11 W. In about 10 miles turn right onto Bowers Hill Road, and make the next left onto Bloomingdale Road toward Gate City. In about 5 miles turn right onto Wadlow Gap Road. Turn right onto US-23 Bus/Main Street. In one mile bear right onto Kane Street. In less than one mile turn left onto West Jackson Street. The Library is a large brick building, ahead on the right. Park on the street.
> **(276) 386.3302   scottpublib.org**

ORIGINAL DOCUMENTS

Scott County Clerk of the Circuit Court has documents and records from 1815. The Clerk and his deputies were especially helpful. All of the marriages have been stored in a unique searchable index on a computer in the record room. Cameras are permitted.

> **FIND IT: 202 West Jackson Street, Gate City, VA 24251** From the Library, continue along West Jackson Street. The Courthouse is ahead on the left. Park on the street. **(276) 386.3801**

GOOD TO KNOW

The Wilderness Trail blazed by Daniel Boone after the purchase of land in what would become Kentucky, passes right through Gate City. **The Fincastle Turnpike** was one of the routes settlers used to reach the Daniel Boone Wilderness Trail. The Turnpike ran through Scott County. Take a driving tour to visit many of the historic attractions of the county. **danielboonetrail.com**

Ferris-Station was the last real way-station for settlers heading to Kentucky from points east through the Moccasin Gap (3 miles south) and the Cumberland Gap (85 miles west) on the Virginia-Kentucky border.

Williams-Mill Dam: The original log dam constructed in the mid-1800s supported the first small corn gristmill on Moccasin Creek.

Lawson Confederate Cemetery is now an officially designated Confederate cemetery and also contains the graves of veterans of many other wars including the Revolutionary War.

Kilgore Fort House built in 1786 is thought to be the oldest building in Scott County. Privately owned, one can get a good view of the Fort from Highway 71.

The Waterfall of Falls Creek can be observed from State Route 65 (Sinking Creek Highway) just north of the Dungannon town limits.

Hanging Rock Recreation Area welcomes hikers, anglers, and has group shelters with tables and grills along with the falls of Little Stony Creek. Two waterfalls.

The Carter Family Memorial Music Center, 3449 A. P. Carter Hwy, Hiltons, VA 24258 includes A.P. Carter's Birthplace, Mount Vernon United Methodist Church and Cemetery, and the A.P. Carter Store—now The Carter Family Museum.

SHENANDOAH COUNTY

The entire Shenandoah Valley was purchased from the Iroquois in the 1744 Treaty of Lancaster. Shenandoah County was formed in 1775 from a part of that land. The name is of Iroquois origin. The county seat is Woodstock.

WHERE TO START

FAMILY RESEARCH

Shenandoah County Library Shenandoah Room and Truban Archives contains resources concerning past and present events occurring in Shenandoah County. The records are available for study within the Shenandoah Room. The Library provides a guide sheet of questions and answers that will aid the researcher.

> **FIND IT: 514 Stoney Creek Blvd, Edinburg, VA 22824**
> Shenandoah County is west and north of Richmond, VA. The most direct route is to follow I-64 west to I-81 north. Exit #279 and follow the ramp about ½ mile. Turn right onto Stoney Creek Blvd. The Library is ahead on the left. There is parking in front.
> **(540) 984-8200   countylib.org**

ORIGINAL DOCUMENTS

Shenandoah County Clerk of the Circuit Court has offices in the Courthouse.

> **FIND IT: 112 S Main Street, Woodstock, VA 22664** From the Library in Edinburg return to I-81 N and travel about 3 ½ miles to exit #283. Follow the ramp and turn right onto VA-42 toward Woodstock. In about ½ mile turn left onto S Main Street. The Courthouse is the red brick building ahead on the left. Watch for the driveway to parking in back just as you approach the building. An alternate route is to take US-11 N. It becomes S. Main Street in Woodstock. **(540) 459.3791**

GOOD TO KNOW

In 2003, the Mid-Atlantic Germanic Society (MAGS) entrusted their collection of over 1,000 books, publications, newsletters and periodicals to the **Shenandoah County Library in Edinburg**. The MAGS library book list: **magsgen.com/library/booklist.**

Shenandoah County Historic Courthouse, 103 N Main Street, Woodstock, VA 22664. It has been restored by the Historical Society of Shenandoah County.

Meems Bottom Covered Bridge, Wissler Road, Mount Jackson, VA 22842 **mountjackson.com**

American Celebration on Parade, 397 Caverns Rd., Shenandoah Caverns, VA 22847 is a museum collection of parade floats, props and stage settings from presidential inaugurals. **(540) 477.4300**

Edinburg Grist Mill, 214 S. Main St. Edinburg, VA 22824 Visit the Mill, the Museum and gift shop.

Our Soldiers Cemetery 1861-1865 Mount Jackson, VA 22842 Burial site of more than 400 Confederate soldiers representing 11 southern states.

Strasburg Museum, 440 E. King Street, Strasburg, VA 22657 Housed in a Southern Railway depot, the Museum exhibits include 18th, 19th, and 20th century pieces and items from Colonial farms, barns, and homes. **strasburgmuseum.org**

The Virginia Museum of the Civil War, 8895 George Collins Parkway, New Market, VA 22844 tells the story of the 1864 Battle of New Market and the Civil War in Virginia. It is also home to the Shenandoah Valley Tourist Center. **(866) 515.1864**

SMYTH COUNTY

Smyth County was formed from Washington and Wythe counties in 1832. The county is named after Alexander Smyth, a general during the War of 1812. The county seat is Marion.

 **WHERE TO START**

FAMILY RESEARCH

Smyth-Bland Regional Library has a local history heritage room that contains a collection to assist library users in researching the history of Southwest Virginia and surrounding areas. Researchers will find census records, county histories and vital records for early inhabitants of the region. Genealogy databases also provide online access to family information and vital records.

> **FIND IT: 118 Sheffey Street, Marion, VA 24354** From Richmond make your way west on I-64 to I-81 S. Exit #45 and merge onto VA-16 N/ S Commerce Street toward Marion. In less than a mile turn left onto E Cherry Street. In about 4 blocks turn right onto S Sheffey Street. The Library is ahead on the left. Park on the street. **(276) 783.2323 sbrl.org**

ORIGINAL DOCUMENTS

Smyth County Clerk of the Circuit Court has court, deed and will records from 1832.

> **FIND IT: 109 W Main Street, Marion, VA 24354** From the Library continue on Sheffey Street and turn right onto US-11/ W Main Street. The courthouse is ahead on the left. There is street parking or take the next left to a parking lot on the side of the building. **(276) 782.4044**

GOOD TO KNOW

Smyth County Museum and Historical Society, 123 East Main Street, Marion, VA 24354. With artifacts, photographs, and manuscripts dating from the early 1800's this "tour through time" reflects the economic and social development of Smyth County and Southwest Virginia
(276) 783.7286

Lincoln Theatre 117 E Main Street, Marion, VA 24354 is a Virginia Historic Landmark. It is one of only three remaining Mayan Revival theatres in America. **(276) 783.6092 www.thelincoln.org**

Marion History Walk 138 W Main Street, Marion, VA
(276) 783.4190

Hungry Mother State Park 2854 Park Blvd, Marion, VA 24354 easily accessible from Interstate 81, this park has folklore and history, swimming, camping, cabin rentals, boat rentals, hiking and the park system's first conference center, Hemlock Haven.
(276) 781.7400 dcr.virginia.gov/state-parks/hungry-mother

The Dip Dog Drive-In on Us-11/Lee Highway near I-81 exit #39 in Marion, VA. The Dip Dog is like a corn dog, but less sweet and with a red hot inside. Best milk shakes in the world! A trip to Smyth County isn't complete without a visit to this hometown place.

SOUTHAMPTON COUNTY

Most of Southampton County was originally part of Warrosquyoake Shire which was renamed Isle of Wight County in 1637. In 1749 part of Isle of Wight County became Southampton County. Later, part of Nansemond County, which is now the Independent City of Suffolk, was added to Southampton County. It may have been named for a major city in England or for Henry Wriothesley, 3rd Earl of Southampton. The county seat is Courtland.

 WHERE TO START

FAMILY RESEARCH

Walter Cecil Rawls Library/Courtland Branch has many genealogy resources including family histories, passenger lists, marriage records, church and cemetery records, indices to wills and deeds and war registers.

> **FIND IT: 22511 Main Street Courtland, VA 23837** From Richmond follow I-95 South to exit #41 and merge around and up onto US-301 N/ VA-35. In about 33 miles this road becomes Main Street. Continue on through town past the Courthouse to the Library on your left. Park behind the building.
> **(757) 653.0298   blackwaterlib.org/courtland**

ORIGINAL DOCUMENTS

Southampton County Clerk of the Circuit Court has original documents from 1749.

> **FIND IT: 22350 Main St., Courtland, VA 23837** From the Library go back into town to the Courthouse. Watch for the parking lot on the left just before the Courthouse as there is limited street parking. Walk from the parking lot, follow the covered archway and turn left to enter the Clerk's Office. There is security screening but only for the Courts.
> **(757) 653.2200**

GOOD TO KNOW

Nottoway Indian Tribe of Virginia's Community House & Interpretive Center, 23186 Main St, Capron, VA 23829 contains a museum with a multitude of Nottoway Indian artifacts.
(757) 653.7932   nottowayindians.org

The Southampton Heritage Village, Agriculture & Forestry Museum, 26135 Heritage Lane, Courtland, VA 23837 is now home to the **Rebecca Vaughn House.** It was the final house attacked during the **Nat Turner rebellion or Southampton Insurrection** that took place in Southampton County in 1831. Visitors can enjoy indoor and outdoor displays and exhibits.   (757) 375.2523   southamptoncounty.org

Civil War Trail Site: Southampton County was home to two Civil War generals…one from each side. General George H. Thomas, the "Rock of Chickamauga", served the Union and General William Mahone, a Confederate, was known as the "Hero of the Crater".
civilwar-va.com/virginia

Historic Courtland Walking Tour: Beginning at the Southampton County Courthouse on Main Street, the free, self-guided tour includes the **Courtland Confederate Monument, Courtland Baptist Church, Southampton Agriculture & Forestry Museum, Mahone's Tavern, St. Luke's Protestant Episcopal Church, Bell House, Seven Gables Home, the Rochelle-Prince House, the Walter Cecil Rawls Library** and end at the **Rawls Museum of the Arts.** Ask at the Courthouse for a map.   (757) 653.2222

SPOTSYLVANIA COUNTY

Spotsylvania County was formed in 1722 from Essex, King and Queen, and King William counties. The county was named for Lieutenant Governor of Virginia Alexander Spotswood. The county seat is Spotsylvania.

 **WHERE TO START**

FAMILY RESEARCH

The Central Rappahannock Heritage Center: The Center archives and preserves historical documents and photographs pertaining to the history and people from the counties of Caroline, Stafford, King George, Spotsylvania and the City of Fredericksburg in Virginia.

> **FIND IT: Central Rappahannock Heritage Center, 900 Barton St., Fredericksburg, VA 22401** From Richmond, drive north on I-95 and exit #130 A. Merge onto VA-3/E William Street. In about 1 mile turn left onto William Street. In one more mile turn right onto Barton Street. The Center is ahead on the right. **(540) 373.3704 crhcarchives.org**

The Central Rappahannock Regional Library Headquarters provides another excellent research site for genealogists and historians. Indices to 1780+ Fredericksburg newspaper obits and microfilm of those newspapers are here.

> **FIND IT: Central Rappahannock Regional Library, 1201 Caroline Street, Fredericksburg, VA 22401** Go back along Barton Street and turn right onto William Street. Go about 5 blocks to Caroline Street and turn left. The Library is 2 blocks ahead on the right at the corner of Lewis and Caroline. Park on the street or behind the building. **(540) 372.1144 librarypoint.org/headquarters**

ORIGINAL DOCUMENTS

Spotsylvania County Clerk of the Circuit Court has most court records including deeds and wills from 1722.

FIND IT: 9115 Courthouse Rd, Spotsylvania, VA 22553
From Richmond follow I-95 N. Exit #126A to merge onto US-1. IN about 1 mile turn left onto Hood Drive. In about ½ mile turn left onto VA-208 W/Courthouse Road. In about 5.5 miles turn left onto Courthouse Road. The Courthouse is 2 blocks ahead on the right. There is parking on the side and in the back of the building. **(804) 507.7600**

GOOD TO KNOW

Spotsylvania Courthouse District was the Battle of **Spotsylvania Court House** which marked the beginning of the fall of the Confederacy. That battle was the scene of one of the bloodiest engagements of the war. General Lee used the 1838 **Spotswood Inn** as an observation point and **Berea Christian Church** was used as a hospital during the fighting. This little church is a fine example of Virginia's Gothic Revival period architecture, and is exceptionally well preserved. The cemetery, located in the rear, dates back to the pre-Civil War period. **visitspotsy.com**

Spotsylvania County Museum, 9019 Old Battlefield Blvd., Spotsylvania, VA, 22553 tells a comprehensive history of Spotsylvania from 1722. The Museum is located on the first floor of the Merchants Square Building across from the pavilion in Courthouse Village. **(540) 507.7210 spotsylvaniamuseum.org**

Lake Anna State Park, 6800 Lawyers Road, Spotsylvania, VA 22553 (800) 933.7275

Spotsylvania Visitor Center, 4704 Southpoint Pkwy., Fredericksburg, VA 22407

STAFFORD COUNTY

Stafford County was formed from Westmoreland County in 1664. It was named after Staffordshire, England. The county seat is Stafford.

WHERE TO START

FAMILY RESEARCH

The Central Rappahannock Heritage Center: The Center archives and preserves historical documents and photographs pertaining to the history and people from the counties of Caroline, Stafford, King George, Spotsylvania and the City of Fredericksburg in Virginia.

> **FIND IT: Central Rappahannock Heritage Center, 900 Barton St. #111, Fredericksburg, VA 22401** From Richmond, drive north on I-95 to exit 130A and merge onto VA-3/E William Street. In about 1 mile turn left onto William Street. In one more mile turn right onto Barton Street. The Center is ahead on the right. **(540) 373.3704   crhcarchives.org**

The Central Rappahannock Regional Library Headquarters' Virginiana Room provides another excellent research site for genealogists and historians. Indices to 1780+ Fredericksburg newspaper obits and microfilm of those newspapers are here.

> **FIND IT: Central Rappahannock Regional Library, 1201 Caroline Street, Fredericksburg, VA 22401** Go back along Barton Street and turn right onto William Street. Go about 5 blocks to Caroline Street and turn left. The Library is 2 blocks ahead on the right at the corner of Lewis and Caroline. Park on the street or behind the building.
> **(540) 372.1144   librarypoint.org/headquarters**

ORIGINAL DOCUMENTS

Stafford County Clerk of the Circuit Court has deeds and wills from 1669.

> **FIND IT: 1300 Courthouse Road, Stafford, VA 22555** From Richmond follow I-95 N for about 65 miles to exit 140 onto Rte 630 toward Stafford and then turn right. The Courthouse is ahead on the left, at the corner of Jefferson Davis Highway and Courthouse Road. **(540) 658.8750**

GOOD TO KNOW

Aquia Church, built in 1757 near Garrisonville, Virginia, is unusual among local structures for having been designed on the plan of a Greek cross. It is still an active Episcopal Church. Listings for the cemetery are available at the website. **aquiachurch.com**

Ferry Farm is George Washington's boyhood home site in Stafford County. **Historic Kenmore plantation** was the home of Betty Washington Lewis, sister of George Washington. **kenmore.org**

Chatham Manor was built between the years 1768 and 1771 by William Fitzhugh. It is a grand Georgian-style house overlooking the Rappahannock River and was for many years the center of a large, thriving plantation. Few houses in America have witnessed as many important events and hosted as many famous people as Chatham. Chatham Manor is now a part of Fredericksburg & Spotsylvania National Military Park.

SURRY COUNTY

Surry County was formed in 1652 from James City County. It was named for the English county of Surrey. The county seat is Surry.

 **WHERE TO START**

FAMILY RESEARCH

The Ann K. & Preston H. Leake Local History & Genealogy Room: The library in Surry is quite small and not equipped for extensive research. The Leake library is located on the 2nd floor of the Appomattox Regional Library, in Hopewell, VA. The room has extensive family files and records about Charles City, Prince George, and Dinwiddie as well as Surry County. This is the best place to begin.

> **FIND IT: 209 E Cawson St, Hopewell, VA 23860** Exit #61A from I-95 South onto VA-10 E/ W Hundred Road. In about 8 miles turn left onto N Main Street and take the 1st right onto E Cawson Street. The Library is ahead on the left. There are two large parking lots adjacent to the Library.
> **(804) 458.6329x2008   arls.org**

ORIGINAL DOCUMENTS

Surry County Clerk of the Circuit Court has land and will records as early as 1645, and court records from 1652.

> **FIND IT: 28 Colonial Trail East, Surry, VA 23883-0203**
> From the Hopewell Library go back to Main Street and turn left, then take the first left onto VA-10 E. In about 30 miles turn left to stay on VA-10. In another mile, turn right onto Colonial Trail East. There is street parking at the Courthouse. Enter through security at the front of the building. The Clerk's Office is on the 1st floor. **(757) 294.3161**

GOOD TO KNOW

Bacon's Castle, 465 Bacons Castle Trail, Surry, VA 23883 is Virginia's oldest documented brick dwelling. It became known as Bacon's Castle because it was occupied as a fort or "castle" during Bacon's Rebellion. It is noted as an extremely rare stylistic example of Jacobean architecture in the New World. **(757) 357.5976   preservationvirginia.org**

Jamestown-Scotland Ferry 16289 Rolfe Highway, Surry, VA 23883. A 15-minute free ferry ride across the James River. **(800) 823.3779**

Smith's Fort Plantation, 217 Smith Fort Ln, Surry, VA 23883. Built between 1751 and 1765, the brick house was home to Jacob Faulcon and his family. The site contains ruins of a fort (1609) begun by Capt. John Smith. A dower tract was given by Powhatan to John Rolfe (1614) upon his marriage to Pocahontas.
(757) 294.3872   preservationvirginia.org

Chippokes Plantation State Park, 695 Chippokes Park Road, Surry, VA 23883 is a 1,947 acre park that offers a combination of natural history, cultural history, and outdoor history. **chippokes.com**

Prior to the Civil War, Surry County had the largest population of freemen in the country. Today, many of these same families can trace their heritage to the Jamestown era of the 1600s and ancestors who were never slaves. Land and cemeteries are still owned by descendants of the original families. **surry.africanheritage.com   (757) 294.5152**

SUSSEX COUNTY

Sussex County was formed in 1754 from Surry County. The county is named after the county of Sussex, England. The county seat is Sussex.

 **WHERE TO START**

FAMILY RESEARCH

The Library in Waverly is the best place to begin as there is no family research facility in Sussex.

Blackwater Regional Library/Waverly Branch offers hundreds of valuable genealogy resources to its patrons. Highlights include passenger lists, court records, marriage records, church and cemetery records, will and deed indexes, and war registers. They also hold many books tracing local family lineage. Contact the Waverly Branch Library in advance of your visit to request specific family information.

> **FIND IT: 125 Bank Street, Waverly, VA 23890** From I-95 S or I-295 S to US-460 S & E. In about 15 miles you will enter the town of Waverly, which has only one traffic light, at the intersection with Rt. 40. Turn right on Rt. 40 at the traffic light and cross the railroad tracks as you travel west on West Main Street (Rt. 40). After you cross the tracks, turn left onto Bank Street. The library is ahead on the left just beyond the Town Hall and the fire station. Park on the street. **(804) 834.2192**

ORIGINAL DOCUMENTS

Sussex County Clerk of the Circuit Court has most deed, marriage and probate records since 1754. Only here can be found a comprehensive individual name index to the Loose Court Papers of Sussex County from 1754 to 1870. This includes all chancery suits (Sussex is not on LVA index for these records) and law suits for that period, as well as petitions, tithable lists, fiduciary bonds and criminal cases. All of these records have been digitized and can be copied by a printer connected to the search computer. Please call ahead to make arrangements to view these files.

FIND IT: 15088 Courthouse Road, Sussex, VA, 23884.
From the Library go back along Bank Street a short way and turn left onto VA-40/West Main Street connector. Turn left again to stay on West Main. In about 14 miles turn left onto Rte 735/ Courthouse Road. The Courthouse is ahead on the right. The Clerk's office is the brick building to the left of the Courthouse. There is parking in front or signs will direct you to alternate parking. **(434) 246.1012**

GOOD TO KNOW

1828 Sussex County Courthouse. This courthouse was completed in 1828 by Dabney Cosby, Sr., who was employed as a builder for Thomas Jefferson at the University of Virginia. The town-hall style of courthouse architecture is evident in this antebellum building.

The Miles B. Carpenter Museum Complex in Waverly is home to the First Peanut Museum as well as the home of **Miles B. Carpenter**, the folk artist who is probably best known for his depiction of the slice of watermelon with a bite taken out of it.

The First Peanut Museum in the New World, 201 Hunter Street, Waverly, VA 23890 tells the story of peanuts through photographs, farm machinery, and equipment.
(804) 834.3327 milesbcarpentermuseum.com

TAZEWELL COUNTY

Tazewell County was formed in 1800 from Wythe and Russell Counties. It was named after Henry Tazewell, a United States Senator from Virginia. The county seat is Tazewell.

 ## WHERE TO START

FAMILY RESEARCH

Tazewell County Library provides an overview of all Tazewell County records and a look at county records that have been transcribed. The Historical Society also has files of family histories. Try to visit both of them.

> **FIND IT: 310 East Main Street, Tazewell, VA 24651**
> From I-81 South exit #72 onto I-77N toward Bluefield. In about 18 miles exit #58 toward toward US-52/Bastian and watch for a left turn onto VA-666/Indian Village Trail. Then in about 1 mile turn right onto VA-614/ Grapefield Road. In about 14 miles keep left to merge with VA-61/ Clearfork Road. In about 9 miles turn left onto Ben Bolt Avenue which will then merge with US-19 Bus/E Fincastle Turnpike. In about 2 more miles (stay with it, almost there!) turn left onto E. Main Street. There is a rock wall in front of the library. **(276) 988.2541 tcplweb.org**

The Tazewell Historical Society

> **FIND IT: 100 E. Main Street** Follow directions to the Library. The Society is on down Main Street on the left. Open on Wednesdays (276) 988.4069, or by appointment.
> **(276) 988.0515   tazewellhistory.org**

ORIGINAL DOCUMENTS

Tazewell County Clerk of the Circuit Court has most court records, deeds and wills from 1800.

> **FIND IT: 101 East Main Street, Tazewell, VA 24651** Follow directions to the Library. The Courthouse is next door to the Library. The Clerk's Office is on the street level. The record room is one floor down. Ask for help when you enter the Clerk's Office. They do not allow photographs of documents.

GOOD TO KNOW

The world's oldest exhibition coal mine is in Tazewell County. The **Pocahontas Exhibition Coal Mine and Museum** is the oldest attraction of its kind, opening in 1938. It is the only Exhibition Coal mine designated as a National Historic Landmark. Adjacent to the Coal Mine is the Coal Heritage Museum (location of the original Power House), Gift Shop, and Educational Room. **pocahontasva.org**

Tazewell County has very distinct geologic areas within the county. **Burke's Garden** is a bowl shaped valley that formed from the collapse of limestone caverns. It is the highest valley in Virginia with only one paved road in. **Burke's Garden** is a small village with a general store, historic churches and beautiful scenery. A Fall festival is held the last Saturday in September. Burke's Garden is also known as "God's Thumbprint". **tazewellcounty.org**

Historic Crab Orchard Museum & Pioneer Park, 3663 Crab Orchard Rd. Tazewell, VA 24651 is a nonprofit comprehensive cultural heritage museum and historical site. The Museum provides living history demonstrations with on-site tours. Demonstrations may be in a variety of areas including seasonal farming chores, drop spindle spinning and wool carding, hearth cooking, use of black powder weapons, and blacksmithing. **(276) 988.6755**

WARREN COUNTY

Warren County was formed in 1836 from Frederick and Shenandoah counties. The county is named for Joseph Warren. The county seat is Front Royal.

 WHERE TO START

FAMILY RESEARCH

The Laura Virginia Hale Archives contain vast amounts of research materials relating to local history from early settlement to the present. The archives office is housed in the rear building behind the Warren Heritage Society's Ivy Lodge Museum and Gift Shop.

> **FIND IT: 101 Chester Street, Front Royal, VA 22630** From I-95 N make your way onto I-66 W. Exit #13 and turn left onto VA-79 S toward Front Royal and then turn right onto VA-55 W. In about 5 miles turn right onto US-522/ S Commerce Ave. In ½ mile turn left onto E Main St. Take the second right onto Chester St. The Museum is ahead on the right. Turn at the driveway just past it to go back to the Archives building. **(540) 636.1446   warrenheritagesociety.org**

ORIGINAL DOCUMENTS

Warren County Clerk of the Circuit Court has complete court records, deeds, and wills from 1836.

> **FIND IT: 1 East Main Street, Front Royal, VA 22630** From the Heritage Society go back down Chester Street and turn right onto E Main Street. The Courthouse is ahead on the left. Street parking is very limited. There is a parking lot behind the Courthouse on Jackson Street. Or take a 4 minute walk from the Archives. Enter the Courthouse from the side that faces Royal Street, turn left and then walk straight back to the Clerk's Office. **(540) 635.2335**

GOOD TO KNOW

Front Royal/ Warren County Visitor Center, 414 E. Main Street, Front Royal, VA 22630 Major tourist attractions include the Shenandoah National Park, Skyline Drive, the Shenandoah River and Skyline Caverns. **(540) 635.5788 discoverfrontroyal.com**

Skyline Drive, **Rte.340 south,** the only public road through Shenandoah National Park, follows the crest of the Blue Ridge Mountains for 105 miles through the park, then joins the Blue Ridge Parkway which connects Shenandoah to Great Smoky Mountains National Park. **(540) 999.3500**

Skyline Caverns, 10344 Stonewall Jackson Hwy, Front Royal, VA 22630, is one of the few places on Earth where rare Anthodites can be seen. The guided tour is excellent. **skylinecaverns.com**

Battle of Front Royal Driving Tour, 414 E. Main Street, Front Royal, VA 22630 (Visitor Center). A guide book is available at the Center.

Warren Rifles Museum, 95 Chester Street, Front Royal, VA 22630 contains as excellent collection of relics and records from the American Civil War. **(540) 635.2219**

WASHINGTON COUNTY

The county was formed from Fincastle County in 1777. It was named for George Washington, who was then commander-in-chief of the Continental Army. The county seat is Abingdon.

 WHERE TO START

FAMILY RESEARCH

The Historical Society of Washington County is headquartered in the old Norfolk & Western Passenger Depot. The Society is the leading center in the region for genealogical and historical research. Call before you visit if possible.

> **FIND IT: 306 Depot Square, Abingdon, VA 24212**
> From I-81 South exit #17 ramp and bear right onto US-58 ALT/ Cummings Street. In less than 1 mile turn left onto West Main Street and take the first left onto Wall Street S. Take the first right onto Depot Square SW. The Historical Society is on the left in the old Norfolk & Western Depot. Park in front.
> **(276) 623.8337   hswcv.org**

ORIGINAL DOCUMENTS

Washington County Clerk of the Circuit Court: The Clerk's Office has a printed guide to the Court records available for research. Most records date to 1777.

> **FIND IT: 189 East Main Street, Abingdon, VA 24210** From the Society go back to Wall Street and turn left. Take the 1ˢᵗ right onto West Main Street. The Courthouse is ahead on the right. There is parking on the street. Walk behind the statue and enter the Circuit Court Clerk's Office through a door to left of the main entrance.
> **(276) 676.6224**

GOOD TO KNOW

Barter Theatre, 127 West Main Street, Abingdon, VA opened on June 10, 1933. It is one of the longest-running professional theatres in the nation.
(276) 628.3991   bartertheatre.com

The Birthplace of Country Music® Museum, 520 Birthplace of Country Music Way, Bristol, TN. 24201 a Smithsonian Institution affiliate, explores the history of the 1927 Bristol Sessions and their lasting impact on the heritage of county music.
(423) 573.1927   birthplaceofcountrymusic.org

Mendota, VA is widely recognized as the Hawk Capitol of the World, and it lives up to its name. Also in Mendota visit the "Barn Rock". A massive boulder provides the wall for an otherwise regular barn, build by Frank Osborne in the 1940s. Notable enough that the road is named after it.

Norfolk & Western Railway Caboose is one of 100 manufactured in August, 1976 by the International Railway Car Company of Kenton, Ohio. Restored in 2009 it now stands proudly in the Depot Square.

Whitetop Mountain is the second highest mountain in the state of Virginia, after nearby Mount Rogers. It is located at the juncture of Grayson, Smyth, and Washington Counties. The mountain is also unique for the fact that it represents an ecological "island" of flora and fauna commonly found much further north than Virginia, such as old growth red spruce and other northern softwoods.

The Abingdon Muster Grounds is the site used by patriot militia in preparation for the Battle of Kings Mountain, South Carolina in 1780. According to Thomas Jefferson, the outcome of the Battle was the turning of the tide of the American Revolution.
(276) 525.1050   abingdonmustergrounds.com

WESTMORELAND COUNTY

Formed from Northumberland County in 1653, the territory of Westmoreland County included the city of Alexandria, Arlington County, Fairfax, and Prince William Counties. These remained Westmoreland until 1664. The county seat is Montross.

 **WHERE TO START**

FAMILY RESEARCH

The Westmoreland County Museum and Visitor Center: This is the best place to begin as the open hours are consistent. Someone is always there to help. They do have family files and other resources available for research.

> **FIND IT: 43 Court Square, Montross, Virginia 22520**
> (Note: the Museum actually faces a new road called Polk Street) From Richmond take I-64 East to exit #192 and merge onto US-360 E. Go about 39 miles into Tappahannock and turn right onto US-360 E/Queen Street. Go about 7 miles and turn left onto Main Street/VA-3 in Warsaw. In less than a mile turn left onto VA-3/History-Land Hwy. Follow VA-3/Kings Hwy for about 12 miles into Montross. Turn right onto Polk Street. The Museum is ahead on the left. Park along Polk Street or turn into the first driveway past the Museum and park in the back.
> **(804) 493.8440   www.inwestmoreland.com**

The Northern Neck of Virginia Historical Society: The Society's library collection includes vital records, family histories, church and cemetery guides, histories of Northern Neck towns and counties, microfilm of the *Northern Neck News*, 1879-1939, and microfilm of the *Virginia Citizen of Irvington*, 1891-1917.

FIND IT: 15482 Kings Hwy, Montross, Virginia 22520. From the Museum turn right onto Kings Highway. The Society is about ½ mile ahead on the left. Watch for a sign out front of a white house. **(804) 493.1862** **nnvhs.org**

ORIGINAL DOCUMENTS

Westmoreland County Clerk of the Circuit Court has wills and deeds from 1653 to the present available for research. Ask for the pages about research in the Record Room.

> **FIND IT: 111 Polk Street, Montross, Virginia 22520.** From the Museum, walk down the block. The Courthouse is ahead on the opposite corner from the Museum. Enter through the front. The Record Room is on the first floor. **(804) 493.0109**

GOOD TO KNOW

George Washington Birthplace, 1732 Popes Creek Road, Colonial Beach, VA 22443 (804) 224.1732

James Monroe Birthplace, 4460 James Monroe Hwy, Colonial Beach, VA 22443. (804) 214.9145

Stratford Hall, 483 Great House Road, Montross, VA 22520 birthplace of Robert E. Lee. **(804) 493.8038** **stratfordhall.org**

Kinsale Museum, 449 Kinsale Road, Kinsale, VA 22488, chronicles life in a vibrant port. Enjoy a walking tour of Kinsale's historic district. **(804) 472.3001** **kinsalefoundation.org**

Northern Neck Farm Museum, 12705 Northumberland Hwy, Heathsville, Virginia 22473. From washing machines, to tractors, sawmills and windmills...it's all at the Northern Neck Farm Museum. Call for appointments. **(804) 761.5952** **nnvhs.org**

A. T. Johnson High School Museum, 18849 King Highway, Montross, VA one of the first African-American high schools in the Northern Neck.

WISE COUNTY

Wise County was formed in 1856 from Lee, Scott, and Russell Counties and named for Henry A. Wise, who was the Governor of Virginia at the time. Wise County shares a border with Lee County in far southwest Virginia. The road which connects Wise and Lee Counties is called Trail of the Lonesome Pine Highway. The county seat is Wise.

 ## WHERE TO START

FAMILY RESEARCH

Wise County Historical Society
For an overview of all Wise County records and a look at records that have been transcribed, start at the Historical Society in the Courthouse in the town of Wise. You will find family files, indexes to transcribed records, and much more to get you started.

> **FIND IT: 206 East Main Street, Wise, VA 24293** Take Exit 17 from I-81 toward Abingdon onto US-58 ALT. Continue to follow US-58 ALT until it merges with US-19 N. In about 12 miles turn left onto US-58 ALT W. In 35 miles merge onto US-23N. In about 3 miles turn right onto US-23 BR/Norton Road. In about 1 more mile turn right onto Main Street. The Society is in the Courthouse building ahead on the right. Park on the street. **(276) 328.6451   wisevahistoricalsoc.org**

ORIGINAL DOCUMENTS

Wise County Clerk of the Circuit Court has court records, deeds and wills from its founding in 1856. There are indices to original records on the main level. Some documents are in a section on the floor below and the stairs are accessed from the record room.

FIND IT: 204 East Main Street, Wise, VA 24293;
The Clerk's Office is in the Courthouse which is on Main Street in the center of town. The Clerk's Office is across the hall from the Historical Society. **(276) 328.6111**

GOOD TO KNOW

The Trail of the Lonesome Pine is a novel written by John Fox, Jr.. It was included on a list of bestselling novels for 1908 and 1909. The movie marked the first time the Technicolor process was used for outdoor filmmaking. The play is performed in an outdoor theater in the author's hometown of Big Stone Gap, Virginia in Wise County.

The Southwest Virginia Museum Historical State Park, 10 W 1st Street N, Big Stone Gap, VA 24219 is an educational facility exhibiting a part of Southwest Virginia's rich heritage. It is housed in an 1888 house made of sandstone and limestone. **(276) 523.1322   swvamuseum.org**

Wise County is on "**The Crooked Road**", Virginia's Heritage Music Trail. **thecrookedroad.org**

Saint Paul, Virginia Town Hall, 16531 Russell Street, St. Paul, VA 24283 is a town on US-58 Alt in the corner of Wise and Russell Counties. "Where the coalfields meet the bluegrass", St. Paul is a place of natural beauty on the Clinch River. The Historic District includes the 1887 Ennis House, and the 1901 St. Paul Hotel.

The St. Paul Loop - Virginia Birding and Wildlife Trail: The Loop offers six excellent sites in proximity to the Town of Saint Paul.

WYTHE COUNTY

Wythe County was formed from Montgomery County in 1790. It was named after George Wythe, the first Virginian signer of the Declaration of Independence. The county seat is Wytheville.

 ## WHERE TO START

FAMILY RESEARCH

Kegley Library at Wytheville Community College: The Kegley Library is a source of local history and genealogy material within the Wytheville Community College Library. Visit the collections section on their web site for a list of holdings.

> **FIND IT: 1000 East Main Street, Wytheville, VA 24382**
> Follow I-81 south to exit #73 and merge onto US-11/E Main Street toward Wytheville. In about 1 mile bear right onto VA-365 which will take you up to the Community College. Follow signs to the Library and parking. **(276) 223.4876 vccs.edu**

Wythe County Public Library: The Wythe County Public Library has special genealogy research areas with extensive reference materials. Among the reference materials are book collections, censuses, and notebooks of locally conducted research.

> **FIND IT: 300 E Monroe St, Wytheville, VA 24382.** From the College head back to US-11/E Main Street and turn right. In about ½ mile turn right onto North 3rd Street. Park in front. **(276) 228.4951 wythegrayson.lib.va.us**

Wythe County Genealogical & Historical Association: The web site indicates it has a genealogy library available for research.

FIND IT: 115 E. Main St, Wytheville, VA 24382 From the Public Library drive on down 3rd Street, turn right onto North Main Street. The Association building is ahead on the right. Park on the street. **(276) 228.2445 wythecogha.org**

ORIGINAL DOCUMENTS

Wythe County Clerk of the Circuit Court has court records, deeds and wills from 1790.

FIND IT: 360 S. 6ᵗʰ Street, Wytheville, VA 24382 The Record Room is not found in the Courthouse. It is in the Circuit Court Building. From the Public Library go back to East Main Street and turn right. Go about ½ mile and turn left onto South 6ᵗʰ Street. The Circuit Court building has brick arches in front. Enter through security, turn right in the lobby to find the Clerk's Office and Record Room. **(276) 223.6050**

GOOD TO KNOW

The **Jackson Ferry Shot Tower**, **176 Orphanage Drive, Foster Falls, VA 24360** is a 75-foot tall structure used to manufacture lead shot for ammunition. Construction began on the tower shortly after the American Revolutionary War. It is one of only three in the United States and may be the only one of its particular design in the world. The American Society of Mechanical Engineers designated the Shot Tower a National Historic Mechanical Engineering Landmark in 1981. It is the centerpiece of the Shot Tower Historical State Park. **dcr.virginia.gov/state-parks/shottower**

The **African American Heritage Museum**, **410 E. Franklin Street, Wytheville, VA 24382** showcases achievements, stories and memorabilia to tell the story of African American education in Wythe County. It is housed in the historic 1882 Wytheville Training School. **(276) 625.0042 wythevilletrainingschool.org**

YORK COUNTY

York County (formerly Charles River County) was formed in 1634 as one of the eight original shires of the Virginia Colony. It was named for James Stuart, Duke of York, who would become King James II. York County is one of the oldest counties in the U.S. The county seat is Yorktown.

WHERE TO START

FAMILY RESEARCH

York County Library maintains a local history room with genealogy information about York County. Here you will find family files, cemetery records, maps and a computer to help with your search.

> **FIND IT: 8500 George Washington Memorial Hwy, Yorktown, VA 23690** Follow I-64 E and Exit #250B around and onto VA-105 E/ Ft. Eustis Blvd. In about 4 miles turn left onto US-17/ GW Memorial Hwy. The Library is ahead on the right.
> **(757) 890.3377   yorkcounty.gov/home/libraries**

ORIGINAL DOCUMENTS

York County Clerk of the Circuit Court has land and will records dating to 1633. Marriage records begin in 1772.

> **FIND IT: 300 Ballard Street, Yorktown, VA 23690**
> From the library continue on US-17/ GW Memorial Hwy about 3 miles. Turn right onto Alexander Hamilton Blvd. Take the 1st right onto Ballard Street and follow it around to the Courthouse parking lot entrance on the right. **(757) 890.3350**

GOOD TO KNOW

Yorktown is one of the three points of the **Historic Triangle of Colonial Virginia**, and the location where victory was accomplished in 1781 at the conclusion of the American Revolutionary War.

The Yorktown Battlefield Visitor Center, 1000 Colonial Parkway, Yorktown, VA 23690 Ranger led tours of the battlefield and historic town leave from the visitor center daily.
(757) 898.2410   yorkcounty.gov

York County Historical Museum, 301 Main Street, Yorktown, VA The old Courthouse building has exhibits highlighting York County's 400-year history; including the Naval Weapons Station, the battlefield golf course, the Coleman Bridge, and the archeology of several local sites.
(757) 898.4910

Grace Episcopal Church, 111 Church Street, Yorktown, VA This original building, built in 1697, continues to serve an active Episcopal congregation. Historic tours are provided on Saturday. Church Services are held on Sunday. **(757) 898.3261**

Watermen's Museum, 309 Water Street, Yorktown, VA 23690 demonstrates the role Chesapeake Bay Watermen, from pre-colonial to modern times, have played in the shaping of our nation. It provides an historical display of exhibits, crafts and methods of their trade, and a look into their lives. **(757) 887.2641**

Other points of interest are included with a National Park Service Admission ticket. Please note these sites are open seasonally as volunteers are available: **Cornwallis Cave; The Moore House; The Nelson House; Poor Potter Archaeological Site; Yorktown Victory Monument.**

ADDITIONAL RESOURCE SITES IN VIRGINIA

Huguenot Society of the Founders of Manakin in the Colony of Virginia Headquarters, 981 Huguenot Trail, Midlothian, VA 23113 has a small library housed in the headquarters of the Manakin Huguenot Society and staffed by a certified librarian during its open hours. The collection of 700+ volumes focuses on Virginia genealogy and history and Huguenot history, with a catalog available on the website. They also have considerable materials, often from member applications, on Huguenots in colonial Virginia, especially at Manakintowne. **(804) 794.5702 huguenot-manakin.org**

The Martha Woodroof Hiden Memorial Virginiana Room at the Main Street Library 110 Main Street, Newport News, VA 23601 contains over 4300 individual volumes specializing in Virginia genealogy and local history including manuscripts, maps, periodicals, photographs, and microfilm on the history of Newport News and Virginia. **(757) 591.4858 nngov.com/library**

The Mariners' Museum Library 100 Museum Drive, New Port News, VA 23606 contains useful information on the ships that brought many ancestors to America. Resources include photographs, ship plans of accommodation, and steamship ephemera The Mariners' Museum Library at Christopher Newport University houses the largest maritime history collection in the Western Hemisphere. The Library strives to make its collection equally accessible to students, researchers and lovers of history.
(757) 591.7782 marinersmuseum.org/library

Norfolk Public Library's Sargeant Memorial Room, 235 E. Plume Street, Norfolk, VA 23510 contains many "how to" genealogy books, private and family papers, court records, county histories, church records, ships' passenger lists, name indexes, and bibliographies.
(757) 431-7429 norfolkpubliclibrary.org

Old Dominion University Special Collections & University Archives/ Patricia W. & J. Douglas Perry Library, 4427 Hampton Boulevard, Norfolk, VA 23529 has manuscripts, including diaries, letters, legal and campaign files, photographs, and maps, that document the Civil War, Virginia politics, military history, African-American history, Norfolk urban redevelopment, women's history, and local history. There are also books and printed material relating to Virginia and Tidewater History.
(757) 683-4483   odu.edu/library/special-collections

Portsmouth Public Library's Esther Murdaugh Wilson Memorial Room, 4427 Hampton Boulevard, Norfolk, VA 23529, is dedicated to the preservation of the history of Portsmouth and its people, and making such information available to interested researchers. The Portsmouth of today includes eight annexations of surrounding areas from Norfolk County; therefore our special emphasis includes many materials about the county and surrounding areas of southeastern Virginia.
(757) 393.8501x 6521
portsmouth-va-public-library.com/local history

Wallace Memorial Room of the Chesapeake Public Library, 298 Cedar Road, Chesapeake, VA 23322 contains **The Norfolk County Historical Society (NCHS) Collection** with materials for use in historical and genealogical research and with emphasis on the City of Chesapeake and the surrounding areas of Southeastern Virginia and Northeastern North Carolina. In addition to research materials, the Wallace Room has a collection of artifacts of local interest on display. The Wallace Room is located on the 2nd floor of the Chesapeake Central Library. **The Virginia Regional History (VRH) Collection** is a newly developed collection of materials provided by the Library. The VRHC covers all aspects of Virginia's history and includes items of interest in the Atlantic coastal region, centered on Virginia. A large variety of books have been collected over the last year to launch this collection.
(757) 410.7147   cheaspeake.lib.va.us

ADDITIONAL RESOURCE SITES IN VIRGINIA

(Continued)

Edgar Brown Local History and Genealogy Collection of the Meyera E. Oberndorf Central Library in Virginia Beach, 4100 Virginia Beach Boulevard, Virginia Beach, VA 23452 holds a comprehensive Local History and Genealogy collection. The 11,000 book collection can be found on the first floor, at the west end of the building. Included in Local History and Genealogy are books, microforms, audio materials and periodicals. There are how-to books, local histories for most of Virginia and some of North Carolina, and genealogical sources for many states. Stop by the Information Desk in the center of the floor.
(757) 385.0150x reference
vbgov.com/government/departments/libraries

Family History Centers

The Latter-Day Saints (Mormons) have the most extensive library on genealogy in the United States. The materials of the main Family History Library in Salt Lake City can be loaned to a local Family History Center. There are significant materials from North America, British areas, Europe, and Latin America and some for other areas. A FamilySearch program is available at each Family History Center. Those individuals who have done research on their family histories can send in their research to be added to the database. The Centers in Virginia are:

Annandale 3900 Howard Street 703-256-5518
Charlottesville Hydraulic Road 804-973-6607
Dale City 3000 Dale Blvd. 703-670-5977
Newport News 901 Denbigh Blvd. 804-874-2335
Oakton 2719 Hunter 703-281-1836
Richmond 5600 Monument Ave. 801-288-1834

Roanoke - see Salem
Salem, 6311 Wayburn Drive   703-366-6727
Virginia Beach 4760 Princess Anne Rd   804-467-3302
Waynesboro – see Charlottesville

Virginia Heritage: Guides to Manuscript and Archival Collections in Virginia is a consolidated database of more than 12,000 finding aids which provide information about the vast array of manuscripts and archival materials housed in historical societies, libraries, museums, colleges and universities across the Commonwealth. This is a great tool for discovering primary source materials documenting the history, culture, and people of Virginia.
vaheritage.org

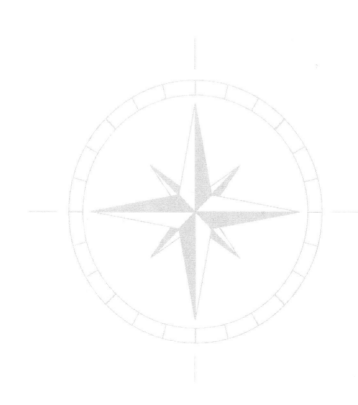

THE NOW EXTINCT
COUNTIES OF VIRGINIA

Beginning in the 1950s, five Virginia cities expanded their boundaries to include the now-extinct counties in which they were geographically situated. **Hampton was once in Elizabeth City County. Newport News was once in Warwick County. Virginia Beach was once in Princess Anne County. Chesapeake was once in Norfolk County. And Suffolk was once in Nansemond County.** Two other cities have become towns again and rejoined the counties in which they are located, **South Boston in Halifax County and Clifton Forge in Alleghany County.**

In 1634 **Elizabeth City** was one of eight original shires. Two years later it was called New Norfolk and two years after that it was divided into two counties: (1) **Elizabeth City County** and (2) **New Norfolk County**.

(1) Elizabeth City County is now the city of **Hampton**. The town of Hampton became a city in 1908 and would eventually merge with Elizabeth City County and the town of Phoebus.
**Record Room, 101 King's Way Mall, Hampton, VA 23669-0040
(757) 727.6105**

(2) New Norfolk County was divided in 1637 into (A) Upper Norfolk and (B) Lower Norfolk.

(A) Upper Norfolk County adopted the name **Nansemond** in 1646. It became the independent city of Nansemond and merged with the independent city of Suffolk. The entire area is now known as **Suffolk**. Records are held at the City Courthouse in Suffolk. Records exist from 1866.
Record Room, Mills E. Godwin, Jr. Courts Bldg., 150 North Main St., Suffolk, VA23439-1604 (757) 514.7800

(B) Lower Norfolk County was divided once again into **(a) Norfolk County and (b) Princess Anne County. (a) Norfolk County** became 3 independent cities. Records of historic Norfolk County are now found in the independent cities of **Chesapeake, Norfolk, and Portsmouth.**
Chesapeake City Courthouse, 306 Cedar Road
Chesapeake, VA 23322. (757) 382.6151
(b) **Princess Anne County** is now the city of **Virginia Beach**. Princess Anne has no existing courthouse but early records are kept at the City Courthouse in Virginia Beach. Land records date to 1691 and will (probate) records to 1783.
Virginia Beach Judicial Center, Building 10B, 2425 Nimmo Pkwy, Virginia Beach, VA 23456   (757) 385.8819

Warwick County, an original Shire is now the city of **Newport News**. Newport News then merged with the city of Warwick. Many court records have been lost.
Newport News City Clerk, 2400 Washington Ave, Newport News, VA 23607 (804) 247.8411

EXTINCT COUNTIES OF VIRGINIA

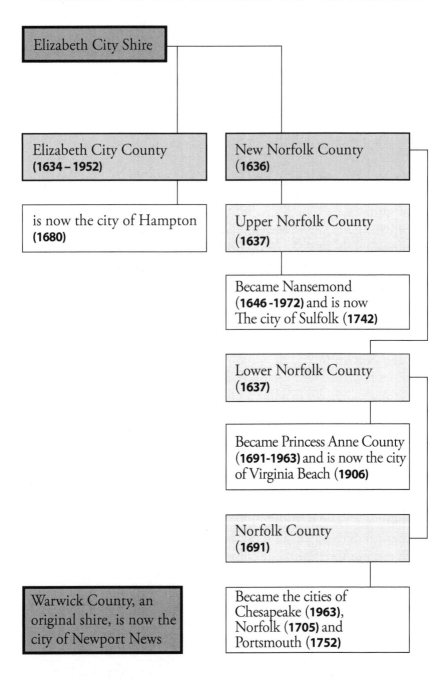

Elizabeth City Shire

Elizabeth City County
(1634 – 1952)

New Norfolk County
(1636)

is now the city of Hampton
(1680)

Upper Norfolk County
(1637)

Became Nansemond
(1646 -1972) and is now
The city of Sulfolk (1742)

Lower Norfolk County
(1637)

Became Princess Anne County
(1691-1963) and is now the city
of Virginia Beach (1906)

Norfolk County
(1691)

Warwick County, an
original shire, is now the
city of Newport News

Became the cities of
Chesapeake (1963),
Norfolk (1705) and
Portsmouth (1752)